RODNEY NAPIER
AND
ELI SHARP

MEETING

Not Just Another

MEETING

CREATIVE
STRATEGIES
FOR
FACILITATION

atd
PRESS

ATD Press is an internationally renowned source of insightful and practical information on talent development, training, and professional development.

ATD Press
1640 King Street
Alexandria, VA 22314 USA
Ordering information: Books published by ATD Press can be purchased by visiting ATD's website at www.td.org/books or by calling 800.628.2783 or 703.683.8100.

Library of Congress Control Number: 2018954244

ISBN-10: 1-56286-688-5
ISBN-13: 978-1-56286-688-4
e-ISBN: 978-1-56286-691-4

ATD Press Editorial Staff
Director: Kristine Luecker
Manager: Melissa Jones
Community of Practice Manager, Learning & Development: Amanda Smith
Developmental Editor: Jack Harlow
Senior Associate Editor: Caroline Coppel
Text Design: Shirley Raybuck
Cover Design: Alban Fischer, Alban Fischer Design

Printed by Versa Press, East Peoria, IL

CONTENTS

INTRODUCTION

After decades as consultants, teachers, and facilitators, we continue to see the need to provide leaders with tools, skills, and strategies for building more effective teams and organizations. Twenty years ago, Rod wrote the first of four books dedicated to translating strategic "designs" into a language accessible to leaders, managers, and particularly facilitators. These simple yet in-depth solution models were designed to help solve a problem, resolve a conflict, make a decision, or address anything else that might block the team, meeting, or organization from reaching a goal.

It should have been a no-brainer: proven ways to improve either team or meeting effectiveness, almost as easy as painting by numbers. However, it took years to discover a certain fallacy in this thinking: Leaders and facilitators would not even attempt our easy step-by-step approach if they had not had the opportunity to experience it firsthand. They had to see the strategic designs being implemented successfully before they would risk trying virtually any of them. The potential for failure or loss of face in front of their direct reports or, heaven forbid, their boss or client would never occur. Rather than chance success, they chose to continue with mediocrity. The keys to victory lay on the table, yet the risk-adverse leader or facilitator would not pick them up.

Suddenly we were faced with huge evidence of the need for a new and innovative way to teach facilitators—and through them, leaders—how to improve their team and meeting effectiveness. So during the latter part of this book, after some brief foundational work, we will bring the experience—the demonstration of our ideas—to you. Learning some accessible new skills should prove to be both interesting and enjoyable as you expand your facilitator repertoire. It will be like shining a new light on situations you've taken for granted for many years; suddenly, you'll have new choices to excite you and your stakeholders. Our job is to make the facilitation process both interesting and fun—yes, fun.

The Extraordinary Dollar Cost of Mediocrity

Over the years, we have conducted several analyses of meeting costs for large businesses that have implications for anyone who has ever attended a less-than-satisfactory meeting. Each time, our rather conservative estimates proved to be mind boggling.

For example, the average executive spends at least 10 hours a week in meetings with an average of five people at each meeting. Each of those individuals would be priced out at no less than $100 an hour, which adds up to $5,000 a week in meeting costs. For larger companies, multiply that $5,000 times 50 weeks, then times the 50 top executives, and the cost is more than $12 million. Yet, of all these executives, only 10 percent said they'd received training in anything more than how to build a meeting agenda. One organization we studied had 300 facilitators at an executive level, and many of the meetings had well over 10 people involved. The associated cost ballooned to more than $100 million a year, with few of the meetings being evaluated, and rarely were the facilitators provided any feedback.

Even more challenging is the admission by a majority of these facilitators that they spend no more than 15 minutes preparing, such as by creating an agenda, for the average one- or two-hour meeting. The reason? They have a limited repertoire of strategies for such meetings other than PowerPoint presentations, or habitually defined approaches that make every meeting seem just like the last one: predictably boring. If you're smiling or grimacing, join the thousands who would agree.

The need, we discovered, is a foundational one—the strategic development of trust and creativity across teams and organizations, through not only design but also the trusted facilitators upon whom organizational leaders depend. Without this strategic development, there are few high-performing teams or truly successful meetings. "Same old, same old" rules, and productivity and innovation suffer with little being done to alter the equation.

For 30 years, we have presented our consulting clients with strategies to facilitate differently, and now we are bringing these tools and skills to you with a new approach that enables you to witness our strategies as if you are in the room. Anyone who reads these pages and studies the accompanying animations will expand their repertoire of facilitation solutions. They'll gain a new understanding of how to work effectively with highly diverse groups of individuals, begin to think diagnostically, and enhance their creativity as facilitators in support of moving teams, meetings, conferences, and gatherings of all kinds to new levels of effectiveness. And the benefits will continue to increase as they become more comfortable with these ways of thinking and acting.

Different Uses of Facilitation

During the past decade, the number of different roles and functions in organizations of all kinds has diminished dramatically, partly because of the economic collapse. The result is an emphasis on the bottom line, staff reductions, and the persistent theme of doing more with less. All three factors have conspired to raise levels of fear and urgency in a crisis-reactive work climate. "Just do it, damn it!" is increasingly the leadership mantra.

Command and control management has returned with a vengeance. More and more leaders have adopted a militaristic, "take the hill" approach. The last thing they want is to be questioned. Community-enhancing behaviors like engagement, collaboration, and open communication, while often discussed, have been shelved because they require precious time both to build the necessary skills and to execute. And there is the lingering fear that working in groups itself requires more time. It is confusing when people still use the words—the cooperative jargon—while doing the opposite. Simply getting people into a room with a demanding topic that shouts out for collaboration and deep discussion will not have a good result, no matter what the boss says. More often than not, the goal of the participants is to finish as soon as possible with a minimum of boredom or pain. A bit cynical, but often true.

Further, leaders are often lulled into believing that facilitation is a simplistic process of formulaic strategies. There are innumerable books pushing their wares on harassed managers, leaders, and their erstwhile facilitators. The "quick and dirty" prescriptive advice promises easy success if basic rules are followed. The 60-Second Leader, or 6 Tips to Success, or Eight Lessons From Genghis Kahn prey on the confusion in leadership today, while also placing greater emphasis on the marketing potential of a concept over its actual content.

Our view is that leadership and facilitation have never demanded so much or been under such challenging conditions. At the same time, never has there been such an array of tools and skills available to improve leadership effectiveness. And facilitators are in the crosshairs of that reality. It is for them to make a silk purse out of a sow's ear. Their leaders tell them what to do and what they expect, but they haven't a clue how to deal with the contradictions and demands thrown at them.

For example, we observed a two-hour meeting with nine executives who were to identify obstacles to their organization's operational efficiency. The meeting facilitator had each of the leaders write down their three greatest priorities and then opened the floor for discussion, dutifully going around the circle of leaders so each would feel involved. Of course, all hell broke loose as the executives argued for the issues that would cause the least disruption to their part of the organization. At the end of two hours, confusion reigned and little knowledge had been transferred, nor was there a commitment to further action.

In our debrief with the frustrated boss and facilitator, we suggested an alternative design that had each of the nine leaders go into one of the areas other than their own and interview 10 floor leaders about what they believed were the greatest operational deficiencies in the organization (not only in their area). The interviewing executive would return with critical issues that blocked organizational efficiencies and that the floor leaders thought needed to be addressed. Then, working in clusters of three, the leaders would identify the five most salient issues drawn from their three groups. Finally, the three groups would come together, making it relatively easy to identify the most critical issues as well as a few salient additional areas that caught their interest.

The design was diagnostic in nature, and it reduced the inherent competitiveness that had corrupted the initial meeting and reinforced the silos that had plagued the organization for years. The facilitator was used to going around the group to ensure that everyone had an opportunity to speak, but the same few leaders tended to dominate every meeting. Thus, the design used at the following session mitigated several deficiencies in the team's working process.

The leader of the executive team hadn't understood the value of the executives listening to the floor leaders, nor the value of the executives working for the good of the whole rather than their own interests. The interview design prepared leadership for eventually doing the heavy lifting necessary to solve the problems the floor leaders raised. Then, even better, the facilitator could engage some of these floor leaders in the problem-solving process. And that, in turn, would increase the probability that solutions would be owned by the floor leaders responsible for enacting them.

For the facilitator, improvement of such a dire situation begins with an awareness of your limitations. So, before digging into the opportunities found in the art of design, it is critical for any facilitator to know how they will affect the group. This means developing the philosophy of "intentional facilitation," the principles of which we'll be exploring. So, in this book, we promise to:

- Provide you with a greater awareness of your impact in your critical facilitation role.
- Add greater rigor and discipline to your role as a facilitator.
- Offer a new way of thinking about the teams and meetings for which you are responsible. We'll also show how even a little additional time designing can enhance the productivity of a group and the individuals who comprise it.

The Purpose of Intentional Facilitation

The role of facilitators in the organizational leadership equation has two equally important sides. The first is being conscious of your own behavioral impact versus your intention. The second is extending your repertoire of what to do and how to do it so that you can respond strategically to any situation with calm, certainty, and creativity. This will forge the necessary trust between you and your leaders. They have handed you the reins for dealing with the widely differing challenges they face every day. As you become more skilled, so will they in their demands and expectations as well as their knowledge of what is possible in any given meeting.

This ability to respond with calm certainty is where the art of design becomes important.

An effective design is not, as you will see, some magical formula. It is a learned set of skills that can change your way of being a facilitator and a leader. Put simply, it demands that you are willing to be both a learner and an experimenter.

As a way of thinking, it's fairly easy to understand. It's based on the belief that virtually every situation demands something to move the team, group, or meeting forward in a positive manner so that those involved feel productive, and, hopefully, well utilized. Now, how many people leave meetings feeling successful, productive, and well utilized? In observing and evaluating meetings for nearly five decades, we've found that the answer is usually very few.

And yet, people do not intentionally create mediocre, boring, unproductive meetings or cultivate combative or passive members of their organization. The truth is that most people facilitating these meetings simply do not ask the right questions as part of the diagnostic narrative we will explore. Nor do they choose the designed activity that will best work for the group. After all, few of their colleagues model what we are suggesting. But our demonstration, through the use of avatars, of the successful designs that could strengthen their limited repertoires can help fill the gap experienced in most organizations.

Successful facilitation is one critical aspect of leadership, just like hiring, creating a compelling vision, or goal setting. It's one way of thinking about yourself in relation to those you lead—it's not as if you can turn off your leadership self at any given time. Intentionality is at the core of successful facilitation. It implies that everything you do is under scrutiny—by yourself and others—and makes a difference in how easily people accept your efforts to lead them through a particular designed activity. Living that simple definition can immediately improve your facilitation effectiveness. It requires no expensive books or seminars, no training program. It demands only a new rigor, a new discipline in how you see yourself and what you do as a facilitator at any moment.

It's like the story of the young father who came to Rod after they'd been working together for a while and asked, "Rod, I have a personal question. My eight-year-old son seems to be afraid of me, gets emotional easily, and feels increasingly distant."

Rod's response, cutting to the chase, was, "Well, what do you do when you're angry with him? After all, you are 6'2" and weigh around 200 pounds."

He paused, as if trying to remember, and said, "We have a good relationship. In fact, I rarely get angry and I can only remember one time when I really lost it. He was five years old and did something stupid and I remember getting in his face and screaming at him. He ended up running out of the room." He added, "I can't imagine he's still carrying that around."

Rod reminded him that at that time, his son weighed, perhaps, 50 pounds, and after watching his seriously angry father fly off the handle, he would never want to see him get that angry again. He added, "Consequently, he has become watchful and cautious and a bit fearful whenever he sees you get red—which you do—and when that telltale vein in your neck starts to pound—which it does—he vacates the premises, emotionally, physically, or both."

Just like the father, most facilitators or bosses become unconscious of their impact and of the signals they emit that say "watch out" or "danger" to others. Other employees, direct reports, or even peers become cautious, especially when they're stressed, and, predictably, defensive. Under duress, pressed, and sometimes unsure of themselves, people become impatient or angry, or perhaps don't feel understood. And, of course, all those little and not-so-little indiscretions are then noted by the individuals who are increasingly fearful of pissing the person off, or potentially losing their jobs. Such caution and fear are cumulative and, over time, can negatively alter a facilitator's effectiveness. And you or other facilitators will likely never be told about your impact. How different is that from the dynamic between the father and his son? He hadn't a clue and he loved his son dearly.

To be a facilitator today is like walking in a minefield, cautious of what you say and how you say it. But, by choosing to be the facilitator, it is your job to be intentional. *What could I do differently to improve the situation the next time?* This becomes your mantra. And, there will be a next time—count on it.

Yes, you can be angry and tell people how you feel. And yes, you can still be spontaneous. Nonetheless, who is to blame for the consequences of your actions? Only yourself, if you believe this way of thinking. That is the challenge. In the complex roles of today's facilitators, these questions are key: *What is your goal in the moment? What is the desired impact for those you lead or facilitate? How do you want people to feel when they leave your presence? Are you up to the level of effort this demands—becoming conscious of both your impact and your intentions?* For many, this is a big order, but an essential one to be the most effective facilitator possible.

Doing Something New as a Facilitator

There are books on fearless facilitation, on facilitating to lead, and on ways of making it easier. Most talk about the *what* of facilitation more than the *how*, and few provide the tools to take you to the next level in your practice. Ours is devoted to the how of facilitation.

In doing so, this book offers leaders 13 classic design modules used effectively by our organization over and over for decades. Each is described in this book, and accompanied by a corresponding animated video (which you can find at www.TD.org/NotJustAnotherMeeting) to visually model the design for facilitators and team members. We believe that seeing leads to doing.

We encourage facilitators to read about the modules, watch the videos, and take notes. With these in hand, the intentional facilitator comes to the conference room ready to inspire increased productivity and creativity within the team and, over time, across the organization.

Following is a table with brief descriptions of the 13 designs. They are provided here to whet your appetite, before their full description (and accompanying illustrations) toward the end of the book.

Solving Problems and Setting Priorities	
Future Search	Each person interviews a group in a method similar to speed dating, with critical findings presented to the whole group in memorable ways.
The Carousel	Small groups rotate through four to six work centers until everyone has responded. Then, the data from each work center are summarized and shared with the larger community.
Collapsing Consensus	Small groups list all the factors causing a problem or ways of solving an issue. Then they join forces with another group with the same problem and negotiate the best solutions (or issues) from the two different group efforts.
Executives and the Common Person	Creates an interview process where deep listening on the part of the leaders provides important information about their team and builds greater trust among those interviewed.
6-Step Problem Solving	This is a stepwise tool for solving problems collaboratively. This problem-solving design is both efficient and interesting, and has wide-ranging applications.
Building Trust and Engagement	
Kings, Queens, and Fairy Tales	By having small groups describe the current reality in the language of Arthurian times, candor and openness are enhanced with doses of needed humor.
Genie in the Bottle	Provides a unique, productive means of teaching and practicing feedback skills.
The 7 in 7	People are asked to share the seven most powerful influences in their lives that have helped make them who they are. This design can have a profoundly positive impact on the trust in a group or team.
The News Conference	Provides a means of overcoming the natural fear many team members have of speaking truth to power. With the leaders also responding to the truth they hear, this can result in positive results at all levels.
Dealing With Conflict	
The 8 and 6	This is used primarily with two members of a team in conflict. It develops a climate where risk taking is shared and relatively equal, resulting in insights for the two parties.
Paradox	Provides participants with new ways of considering conflict, especially when it deals with difficult people. It looks at how the problem solver can unintentionally become the perpetrator.
Questions, Only Questions	Can help move a "stuck" team, group, or committee forward by resolving what ails them in real time.
Speak Out	Legitimizes strong feelings (such as issues around race, ethnicity, or gender) through deep listening, with a goal of understanding differences rather than striving for specific answers.

Understanding the why and how of each design results in confidence that can be felt by those being led. It's like the satisfaction gained when the last pieces of a complex puzzle fall into place. In the process, you as the facilitator will begin to feel more confident in creating your own designs based on the needs confronting you. By accurately assessing the need of the group in the moment and understanding design, you will find choices materializing almost instantly. Seeing a design as a creative act opens possibilities that may never have been considered. Witnessing the design unfold before your eyes transforms this learning process from one of telling you about facilitation to the exploration of new possibilities that will stimulate both you and those you facilitate.

The marriage of intentional facilitation and design should, at this point, be easy to understand. It is the specificity of intention, based on an incisive diagnosis, that drives design. It is for us to put the necessary meat on the bone of that principle that, in turn, provides the lessons of this book.

Most facilitators run their meetings and efforts to engage groups on the fumes of old habits and routines that have lost their meaning and zest. They reflect the remnants of boring teaching translated into boring meetings. Who, for example, has not gone to a weekly meeting that is completely predictable in how it begins, how it ends, how any discussion is conducted, and who talks and who doesn't, along with the knowledge that there won't be sufficient time to complete the agenda? Equally predictable is that those participating in the meeting will leave frustrated at best and angry at worst. To compound the problem, the facilitator, predictably, will virtually never seek or receive feedback about the perceived waste of time many people feel. It reminds me of those who have sat through a horrendously boring sermon in church and proceed to congratulate the minister on their way out on the wonderful service. The same thing often happens to meeting participants who survive a similar experience and then commend the boss or the facilitator for a job well done. One thing's for certain: When we talk about engagement and a stimulating meeting, we will rarely find the answer in a presentation slide deck.

As a result, the first few chapters of this book will equip you with a new way of thinking and acting intentionally when facilitating meetings and working with teams. The second half of the book provides the following:

- It introduces you to 13 creative designs, using animation to demonstrate how to successfully implement the strategies.
- It allows you to experience each design on a visceral level in a risk-free environment, which will increase your confidence and motivation to use the new approach.
- It reminds you how adult learners learn, so you can enhance engagement and encourage them in your efforts to create your own inventive designs.

By using new animated technology to illustrate these designs, along with new communication strategies, we hope to spread the word among those inspired to bring creativity to their workplace and to groups of all kinds.

We expect to help all our readers bring interest, creativity, and effective outcomes to the workplace. To this end, the concepts of personal impact, intention, and design are highly correlated. The good news is that it begins with your willingness to break some old, habitual ways of acting. This book will help you expand your own possibilities every time you are faced with a group, team, or individual that demands something more than same old, same old and, as a result, will bring out the best in you. If you truly understand and use these concepts, you will never be boringly predictable or run out of possibilities.

ACKNOWLEDGMENTS

I want to thank Amma, Laura, and Tori—my three beautiful daughters—for the extraordinary support I have felt over these many years. They've given me loving space to do my work, sometimes at their expense. I hope they have felt my sincere efforts to live the values and skills about which I have written.

—Rodney Napier

To my love, Vincent. Thank you for your never-ending support and true partnership on our journey together.

—Eli Sharp

PART I

DESIGN AND PREPARATION

What do I want to do? » How am I going to do it?

The first section of this book introduces the concepts of intervention, intentionality, and meeting design both in facilitation and in everyday life. It will help you organize your thoughts with respect to what you actually want from your team, how you want them to feel during your initiative, and where they are starting from.

There are a series of diagnostic questions to help you assess the current situation, and another to help you understand your facilitation behaviors. The concepts are introduced with stories from our experiences that will give you a solid grasp of how facilitation works both in real time and over time. We assume you are starting from the beginning, and ours will be a developmental approach to the notion of design.

1

THE ART OF DESIGN

For 35 years, we conducted a leadership development program in the wilds of Ontario, Canada, on Lake Temagami. People would fly in on a bush plane and stay between 10 and 15 days to learn how to be more effective leaders and facilitators as they attempted to create a high-performing community. The 16-20 participants took pseudonyms and shared none of their back-home realities, such as the nature of their work role, authority, or background. In addition, we used many Native American rituals to encourage participants to step out of their habitual and predictable back-home cultures and ways. For example, participants spent hours sitting alone in deep woods, listening to and observing the transition between day and night. There were team-based problems to solve and decisions to make that demonstrated how individuals coped with time-driven stress. Participation in Native American sweat lodges tested their courage and ability to be vulnerable. And community meetings provided the stage on which individuals shared some of their challenges—how they were stuck or needed to be different when they returned home. Thus, risking became the norm, with more curiosity and openness expected with each new day and experience.

As the program unfolded, the growing trust among team members allowed them to try on new behaviors and eventually receive critical feedback. The participants hailed from a wide range of white- and blue-collar professions, including physicians, teachers, business executives, managers, therapists, electricians, and carpenters. People came expecting to be challenged physically, emotionally, and spiritually, with many concerned about the "Who am I now?" question that people need to ask periodically throughout their lives, but seldom have the time to do in our 24/7 world. The sweat lodges, vision quests, and other designs created an environment as challenging as it was inspiring.

By the end of the first week, after sharing some powerful experiences, participants fell into the expected pattern of emphasizing victories and minimizing discord, quickly bonding into a seemingly tight-knit community in what many would call the honeymoon phase of the group's development. As leaders, it was our role to introduce an event or experience that would compel the community to deal with real conflict, much of which, if you knew where to look for it, simmered under the surface. Being averse to conflict had become the norm, as it often does in many business communities. For example, normally, several cliques would have emerged in such a temporal community, and some individuals would feel left out, or personality issues among the participants would be magnified as differences in power and authority within the developing community.

But politeness continued to rule, and being authentic often took a back seat to members wanting to appear both open and together. When the desire to be "members" begins to trump honesty, mistrust begins to creep into the group just as it does in an office, club, or even church community. The result is that conversations can become contrived and superficial as unspoken feelings and issues are not dealt with. In a community that outwardly prided itself for creating trust, spontaneity, and authenticity, caution, doubt, and suspicion were evolving—none of which result in a climate where deep personal learning is really valued. And that was the reason most said they came to this wilderness setting in the first place. Put bluntly, hypocrisy and insincerity were on the rise.

With this in mind, during the sixth afternoon at lunch, we asked how many vegetarians there were who would not eat chicken. We asked early because the group would be involved in intense activities leading up to dinner, and the leaders were responsible for meeting the dietary needs of the group. Three people, including one of our facilitators, were strict vegetarians, with two others saying they had been experimenting with not eating chicken or beef during the program.

By 6 p.m., having engaged in several physically challenging and rather emotional activities, the group had come together in an opening in the forest prior to dinner, to process the day's events. The 18 participants were spread out in a large, irregular circle.

Inside the circle were two crates, which contained four squawking chickens. Next to the cages were a sharpened ax and a 10-inch knife. The group was told that the chickens were to be part of a chicken stew and that a pot of vegetables had been set aside for the two vegetarians so they could be part of the experience.

The incredulous momentary silence did not last long. One person said they would never eat chicken again if they were going to have to kill the "little beasts." Someone else shouted that it was hypocritical to eat poultry from sanitized cellophane packaging but not be willing to undertake the deed itself. However, nobody was volunteering to actually kill them. Things rapidly deteriorated: Some individuals invoked religious beliefs concerning killing, and one recalled the childhood trauma relating to the "murder" of a favorite pig that led him to a life as a vegetarian. It was not a pretty sight as brewing interpersonal differences bled into the chicken conversation and people stood firmly by positions that had never before been challenged. Snickers, tears, and insensitive words were tossed out. The program leaders, predictably, were criticized by several of the group members for placing them in such an uncomfortable position—as if comfort was one of our goals.

As a result of this quite intentional design, the group's aversion to conflict was breached, and the value in the event identified. Even though many still resented the activity, this essential design demonstrated the difference between nice and polite assertions versus authentic expressions that revealed who people really were. It was both fascinating and rewarding to have the group own up to how many of them had chosen to be less authentic since coming together for the program. Before the chicken challenge, they had carefully monitored unspoken pacts so that budding friendships were not disturbed and their membership in the group could be preserved. It sounded to us like most organizations and "teams" with whom we often consult.

The community members also agreed that unresolved conflicts exist in nearly every group, which opened up a discussion about how these pent-up frictions could, inevitably, result in dysfunctional norms and attitudes that, over time, can diminish trust and candor. The intervening chicken design uncovered secrets and unmet needs that were waiting to escape. In the aftermath of the first explosion, the community resolved their differences, began to discuss previously unmentioned tensions, and designed solutions acceptable to the group in relation to killing, dressing, cooking, and, yes, celebrating the chickens. There was little doubt that the group would never be the same—and they would most likely never approach leading their own teams in the same light again. As facilitators, we completed a natural cycle of diagnosis (what did the group need at this time), risk in committing to a design to move the group forward, and evaluation of our effectiveness in that process, which would set the table for our next designed activity based on where the group appeared to be in terms of their needs and our goals.

Essential Factors of Successful Design

A successful design, of course, is a planned design. Without planning, it can quickly devolve into a mess, which is *not* what the intentional facilitator desires. Let's dive into the anatomy of the Great Chicken Challenge to understand the important factors to consider when approaching your own design, whether the design component is for a single-agenda meeting or one part of a multistage event.

The specific goal of the Great Chicken Challenge was to generate authentic, candid behavior within the budding team's dynamic, whether or not they were pretty and polite. All designs share a common goal, however: to better utilize people during any meeting. To achieve that critical goal—our intention—we have learned to pay attention to seven factors that are essential in any successful design and guide our actions. Table 1-1 lists these factors, along with key questions to consider. We discuss them in detail in following pages.

Table 1-1. Seven Factors Critical for Design Creation

1	2	3	4	5	6	7
Task	Process	Variables	Benefits	Challenges	Accountability	Follow-Up
What is the need?	What is the desired level of engagement?	How much time is needed?	What are the positive outcomes desired?	What could go wrong?	Who is accountable (and for what)?	How will the outcomes of the design be monitored?
What is the desired product?	How should individuals feel during the design?	Who will be present?	What is the value added?	Could there be any unanticipated consequences?	What are the measures of success?	How will we evaluate the design itself?
What is the problem to solve?	What is the physical setting?	What is the time of day?				
What decisions need to be made?	Is there any conflict or unfinished business?					

Task

When people come together to work, there are both task and process dimensions. Task has to do with the achievable goal and the actions necessary to reach that end. Often this is a problem to solve, a position to be argued, or a set of choices to make. The actions emanating from this task—the process—should result in satisfying the identified need. This need is the "what" or goal of the work equation: the desired outcome. In the Great Chicken Challenge, our desired outcome was to crack the egg of conflict aversion still holding the group captive and making them unwilling to be open and authentic. We didn't know exactly how the scene in the forest would play out, because the group would have to fend for itself: Deal or not deal with the new dilemma that was rocking their reality. However, we predicted the group would leave the honeymoon stage of their group development and, hopefully, become more productive, honest, and authentic with one another. These, in turn, are the keys to real trust.

Process

Process is the sibling of task; however, since the global recession of 2008, bottom-line tasks have been the corporate mantra. The "what" of work—task—has continually trumped process—the "how" of work. This is true even though morale, productivity, and turnover are tied at the hip to process and, ultimately, to profits. Fear is the driver of this short-term, reactive management.

Balancing the what with the how is why people need conscious facilitators—and it's the focus of a lot of design work. It is central to the notion of "engagement," which is spoken and championed much more than it is lived or understood. Prior to the chicken exercise, what was not being said was debilitating to the cohesion and trust of the group, allowing superficiality to rule like it does in most relationships. In this instance, the program leaders decided to deal with this uncomfortable reality by utilizing the chicken design. This meant breaking the superficial, unspoken goals (or norms) of niceness and politeness with a challenging task that would force the group to look at the "how" of the task, the killing and dressing of the chickens. Once that task was accomplished, the group could use the successful experience to access the "how" of the group's relationships, discussions, and decision making in other areas. Thus, we designed a laboratory for looking at such issues, a crucible of our making for the group's learning and development. Our intention was to force such engagement, which we hoped would lead to greater honesty and trust. Such opportunities to learn from each other rarely occur in the rushed and time-bound world of most organizations. The result are cultures where planning and conflict resolution are often avoided and crisis reaction thrives.

As facilitators, you also know many groups where superficiality rules. In these groups, conflict goes underground, and risk taking is, at the very least, limited. As a result, people often do not hear what they need to hear, especially if the speaker fears such messages will end up being criticized. Carefully planned intentional designs seek to upset any dynamic that compromises trust. Therein lies the creativity of design and the challenge to the facilitator to move the group forward. The chicken activity was a risk for us because we could not control the response of the group and knew it would alienate some in the process. We also knew that talking to the group intellectually about their rising aversion to conflict would not change that reality. One can begin to see how we needed both task and process to be aligned if the design was to be successful.

Variables

While never ideal, the givens or variables often define a situation and have a large impact on what is possible from a design perspective. An available budget, a limiting timeline, unresolved conflict in a team, past failures or successes, and strong personalities in the mix are typical variables at work that influence a situation. These factors need, at minimum, to be considered with their consequences anticipated. This fact prompts increased complexity in the facilitator's thinking and eventual acting. In the chicken situation, we were limited by the time of day and time available to do our design. We were limited by the nature of the physical space, although we intentionally moved the group away from the comfort of the camp itself. We were also limited by our fear that the group would not see the relationship between the extreme design and the dysfunctions within their group. The consequence might be the alienation of the group with one another and us. There is a certain comfort that comes from living in ignorance, and denial is the easiest way to maintain such comfort. After all, it requires courage, honesty, vulnerability, and work to overcome the natural deceptions and dishonesty that are perpetuated, often for years, within some teams, committees, and even families. As facilitators, we took the risk in favor of candor, openness, and trust in the service of authenticity.

Benefits

Like in any venture, if the benefits of the desired outcome don't outweigh the risks, it would be a good idea to run. But this requires a certain hard-nosed scrutiny of reality and the willingness to diagnose both the benefits and challenges to the team. Normally, benefits are translated into profits, increased morale, continued work opportunities, or measured trust. In theory, every time a facilitator takes an hour of their team's collective time, the outcome should increase some of these factors, which perhaps stimulate curiosity, lead to a success of some kind, or generate useful information or the solution to a problem. But, instead, often meetings are predictably boring, proving to be of little value to the participants. Imagine the influence this has on morale and participation, as members bide their time until the end. Then they leave with the less-than-ideal feeling of relief. And that is what they bring to the next meeting. With all the stress our chicken design created for the group, we thought the benefits would push the group to a new and necessary level of both trust and effectiveness.

Challenges

For every action there is a reaction. Your job as facilitator is to presuppose the reaction to everything you do. If there are potential negative consequences to a design, what are they? Can they be overcome? Do the benefits outweigh the challenges? How do you overcome skepticism or fear among the team, and turn their uncertainty into confidence? How is a recent failure translated into a learning opportunity instead of guilt or shame? Motivating the unmotivated is a challenge, as is learning from a failure or just considering unanticipated consequences for any action the team takes. Was the band of participants gathered in Temagami with us ready to handle their own dysfunctions and leave behind the unrealistic norms guiding their group and limiting their progress? Would the small window of time between 6 and 9 p.m., when darkness takes over, be sufficient to bring the necessary closure and healing to the predictable stress we created? Could we find the necessary chickens in an area where few exist because of the cold winters? Had we provided the group with the skills to pull off their own recovery once the lid was blown off the tight container of conflict aversion? All these issues needed to be addressed.

Accountability

In your experience, how often have meeting participants promised to accomplish certain tasks by a certain date or by the next meeting? And how often are apparently good ideas discussed during a meeting, then later dismissed by participants after they've promised action? There is nothing more demoralizing than promises not being kept by some, and this influences the work of others who did keep theirs. Not only are promises often not kept, but rarely are there any consequences as excuses and blame come to the rescue of those who have not been held accountable. Any good design needs to have built in accountability. When teams don't trust each other, aren't open to feedback, or fear alienating their peers or their bosses, a lack of accountability will surely follow.

This was such a risky and pivotal design for the life of this group, we had to have contingency plans in case the group imploded and recovery was not happening as we had hoped. As the planning team, we were accountable; we had to be prepared and on the same page, recognizing plenty of room for failure. Trust had to be absolute. Thus, accountability among us was critical in both the real-time application of the design and the follow-up. Follow-up is important enough to have its own category.

Follow-Up

Didn't we agree to that before? Wasn't that Jim's to undertake? Didn't we lay out that plan in October? The failure of accountability will undermine any effort. Without agreed-upon, specific follow-up—and without identified, measured outcomes—success will be short lived. That said, people often live with unfulfilled commitments with no consequences. The result can be a slow degrading of trust. Thus, we have to ensure accountability to the measured outcomes, creating follow-up and monitoring activities that include tracking commitments. This is a critical part of any team or design. Assessing consequences and addressing them, if necessary, is key to any facilitation. Hard-nosed critiquing is essential to this and what occurs next.

Our chicken design was not a "one and done" event. The results would reverberate for the next nine days of the group's life. It provided us with rich information that would drive us as well as the group forward. Obviously, it was tied closely to accountability. It was also a perfect example of how an intervention in one area can influence the rest of the "system" as it moves ahead and develops. Thus, personal relationships within the group would be influenced, as would the trust toward us and among the rest of the participants. And, if other unanticipated consequences of the design arose, we had to be prepared to deal with them. For example, once the group decided that it wanted to be more open and forthcoming, committed to dealing with conflict as it arose, it was essential not to let the group go back to sleep.

The facilitators could not permit them to revert to ignoring conflict as it raised its head, which it surely would. As suggested previously, good intentions will not drive change by themselves. New rigor and discipline among the group must be cultivated consciously, probably alongside new ground rules and built-in guidelines regarding feedback. All that demands more work, more courage, and more commitment among the members. It would be just plain easier to return to the old patterns of denial, avoidance, and superficially nice relationships—which is exactly why facilitators are needed and, among other reasons, we wrote this book.

Facilitation and Design

If you keep these seven factors in mind as you create designs to build team cohesion and productivity, they will soon become as natural as any habitual aspect of leadership or management. Each step will flow easily into the next. And, as you commit yourself to utilizing interesting and creative designs, your repertoire, along with your courage, will expand. That is the challenge: to internalize the steps until they change the way you see the team or the meeting, while gaining the confidence to risk even more creatively.

As facilitators increase their diagnostic skills and extend their repertoire of tools, they realize that designing ways to move a team or system forward is a creative act. There are no boilerplates, no predesigned formulas for what to do. Instead, facilitators ask, "What can I create that will benefit the group, overcome resistance, or accelerate the work as a team?" And, at the same time, "Can I make the activity more fun or interesting—or both?"

To set you securely on that path, as promised, 13 classic designs are provided in the second part of this book. Through them, you will learn how to develop carefully designed activities and strategies that are meant to elicit specific constructive behaviors from people: to legitimize their sharing of emotions and feelings, confront hard realities, solve difficult problems, and better understand the complexities of groups, teams, and entire organizations.

Designing will often feel like plotting an expedition. It's serious work that demands meticulous attention. In the extreme, it's like Ernest Shackleton and the crew of the *Endeavor,* stranded for two years with temperatures often below −40 degrees, hopelessly lost without sufficient food or clothing on the Antarctic ice floe, their ship having been crushed by the relentless ice. But, in the end, and because of the crew's courage and Captain Shackleton's leadership, not a single man was lost. Captain Shackleton had most of the skills we have identified. His men loved him, yet he was incredibly rigorous and meticulous in everything he did. And, every-thing he did had consequences for which he was accountable, whether doling out grog for a party to lift the crew's failing spirits or bringing ordinary seamen into the decision-making process. He patiently and strategically "designed" their survival and their escape from certain death. Virtually everything he did was intentional and visible to his crew.

In today's business world, the thinking is the same, albeit the consequences less severe. It's a disciplined way of both thinking and acting about every action you take as a facilitator.

2

INTENTIONAL FACILITATION IN ACTION

The rigor and commitment underlying the notion of intentional design did not begin with the chicken design in the Temagami wilderness. It occurred as a result of several disconnected experiences that, together, at the end of many years, revealed themselves to be foundational to the very notion of being a facilitator. They had powerful implications for us as facilitators, teachers, and consultants, and remain central to most of our work. The brief stories that follow spell out the critical dimensions of intention and design. They were unforgettable to us and, hopefully, they will work their way into your psyche as well.

The Terrifying Sergeant Hatchel

The seeds of intentional facilitation, unbeknownst to Rod, were planted deep within his soul nearly 50 years ago by Sergeant Hatchel, a man known by many of Rod's equally fearful fellow recruits at the time as the nastiest, meanest drill instructor in the entire United States Marine Corps.

Sergeant Hatchel took no prisoners. A machine gunner, he had fought in two wars and was looking for a third—with us. His permanent scowl said, *Never make a mistake and we can live together—but, even then, I won't like it and I will never like you.* When he was around, we lived in perpetual terror. He was bound to find imperfection.

It was a sweaty, torrid day in July in the last place anyone would want to be: Parris Island, South Carolina. As a wet-behind-the-ears recruit, I had somehow been anointed a squad leader whose main job in life was not to piss off Sergeant Hatchel. Even worse, any mistakes of the small band I led became my mistakes and oh, how I would pay. As a result, I was always on full alert—that is, almost always.

On that particular July day, I was ushering my 12 privates back to the barracks after a grueling two hours of physical training under an unforgiving, broiling sun. Stopping perhaps 25 yards from the barracks, I casually looked back over my shoulder at my weary group. Without even a wave, I shouted, "Group, dismissed."

From a second-floor window came a screaming tirade: "Private, you get your sorry ass up here or I'll come down there and break your miserable neck." It was Sergeant Hatchel looking for blood. My blood.

Needless to say, I ran to the small porch in front of the barracks to receive his rage and the punishment to come. He was just warming up. "What do you think you are doing—taking a walk on the beach? That kind of slovenly, undisciplined behavior is what gets people killed, and you'd be the cause of it."

Not pivoting smartly and saluting while giving my order was my sin.

His rant continued as he proceeded to insult me, several of my favorite body parts, and my closest relatives, all the while asking me why I had the nerve to insult the entire Marine Corps by joining in the first place.

Between gritted teeth he shouted, "I want 200 squat thrusts, 200 sit-ups, and 200 push-ups, 25 at a time, and then we'll see what else. And they had better be perfect!" A rush of adrenaline drove me through the first six rounds of 25, in spite of my exhaustion. And then, there was nothing left to give. Meanwhile, he was screaming something about me being a spineless chickenshit. He had me stagger to my feet, stand up, heels angled against the wall, body pressed straight against it. From there I was to slowly lower my body and hold it halfway down. Well, my entire body was shaking in a matter of minutes. I caught a glimpse of his sneering smile.

Sometime later—I had lost all sense of time and my body—he screamed, "Private, when I count three, I want your sickening self out of my sight!" When three came, I couldn't move. I didn't even feel pain, just fitful humiliation and a commitment to pay full attention in the future. All these years later, it's still there— that huge gift from Sergeant Hatchel: Pay attention. Be fully present. Own your own mistakes.

The lesson, in my words: Be intentional in everything you do as a facilitator, because there are real consequences for yourself and others. There are few shortcuts and no six-easy-steps to success.

Somewhere in most of our lives we've all been blessed with our personal Sergeant Hatchel. It might have been a teacher, a coach, a ballet instructor, a librarian, or even a Zen master; someone who was there and who cared enough to demand the best from you because it makes a difference.

While Sergeant Hatchel was a terror to any young recruit, he knew his role and, thankfully, was unforgettable in it. In fact, he facilitated our hellish journey through boot camp so we would survive and become the marines he hoped we would be.

Although I believe the "how" can differ (it doesn't demand actual suffering), the message is clear. Facilitation demands a meticulous and rigorous approach to "what" is expected of us in any given moment. And, how many facilitators do you know who act like this and are fully committed to it? I am sure that my three daughters could have done with a little less of the Sergeant Hatchel in me, but I believe the benefits of such an attitude far outweighed my occasional fatherly outbursts.

Disinterested, Reluctant Students

As a novice assistant professor at Temple University 40 years ago, Rod was part of a new department exploring an entirely new field of study: group dynamics. One of his duties was to teach learning theory at the university's Tyler School of Art, to arts students who were decidedly uninterested in anything he had to say. It was a requirement few desired.

Originally trained as a therapist, it took me until the end of my training to discover that I was not meant to work with depressed people for the rest of my career. So, with a newly minted PhD and nowhere to go, quite by accident, I stumbled upon the world of group dynamics. Luckily, I loved what they did and had a knack for it. That said, I had embarrassingly little knowledge of the department's ins and outs, although it was only their second year of operation and they were learning as well.

As a department (one of only three such departments in the United States), we had certain institutional obligations. One was to instruct students at Temple's famous Tyler School of Art—a social science requirement—in this case, in learning theory. It was a distraction for any student studying art, and it demanded of me a 10-mile ride from the main Philadelphia campus to face students who were no more interested in learning theory than in the man in the moon. As the newest, least-tenured faculty member, I was handed the assignment and told to make the experience as painless as possible for both them and me. Some of my colleagues laughed out loud at the "opportunity" I was being given to test my limited teaching skills. I had no idea what they meant. One of my colleagues even said, "Think of yourself as a facilitator and you'll be fine." In those days, facilitator was not in my limited repertoire.

It couldn't have been worse. The classroom was six rows across and 15 rows deep, with 30 students scattered throughout the 90 seats in a variety of slouching reposes that said, *This is going to be a stupid waste of time, and there is nothing I can possibly learn from you that could be of any interest to me. I want to be in the art studio, working on something meaningful.* To make matters worse, the assigned text had been written by a scholar attempting to be scholarly, with no interest in applying the learning theories he espoused in his own book about learning. If toast is dry, this was with sand as butter. It was a disaster waiting to happen.

The 12-week course met for three consecutive hours once a week, at 1:30 in the afternoon—known as the teacher's dead zone. What could be worse for all of us? They were reluctant students, right after lunch, full of food and disinterest.

I did what I knew (certainly not much about learning theory). I lectured about learning. University art students have amazing ways of expressing themselves when something is not only dysfunctional, but also boring and unrelated to anything that might resemble their interests. They came late, left early, slept, ate, drew in their notebooks, and did other homework as I droned on. After the first six hours, witnessing the continued deterioration of morale, I was embarrassed for them and myself. It was pathetic. It reminded me of my worst classes in college, times 10. Now, I was the perpetrator. I wanted to blame them for their disrespectful behavior, but I couldn't.

Then, brilliantly, I thought, *What's more interesting for 19-year-olds than themselves?* How we learn could be related to almost everything we do, whether it's managing change, relationships, or in their case, their own unsettled views of themselves. Moreover, they knew far more about themselves at 19 than I did. Getting them talking about things of interest to them was the key.

I used the text as a reference, used another simpler applied text for myself, and began asking questions about everything. Instead of being stuck, I revived myself. Instead of drowning in self-pity, I explored ideas that fascinated me, assuming that if I found a topic compelling, I would be better able to excite them. The result was that I began to hear laughter first from the small discussion groups and later from the larger class and, then, even from myself. I engaged them in their own learning and in their exploration of themselves as young adults with young adult problems that could then be related to theory and research.

I used the absurdity of our own situation and how I had begun, breaking every rule of learning theory, when teaching learning theory. We learned and we had fun. I asked them in groups of three to think of the best and worst learning experiences they'd had (other than mine) in the past year and the advice they would give the teachers of the latter course if they had the opportunity. It was humbling how much they actually knew about learning. Then I asked them to write a two-page paper blending their insights and those of some other classmates and relate them to some of the theory outlined in the text. Instead of the text making them feel ignorant, they felt smart and authoritative as a result of their own observations. Toward the end of the course, in new groups of four, they had to create a David Letterman–style *Top Ten List of Dos and Don'ts for Anyone With the Nerve to Teach Learning Theory to 19-Year-Olds*. Each item had to be supported by either theory or research. I then blended their insights into a small booklet called *Truths From the Mountain* that I related to key learning concepts—and that I used the second time I taught the course.

Without knowing it, I had, by asking myself hard questions about every aspect of this "teaching nightmare," introduced myself to a diagnostic mentality and then to the art of design. I had to create the answers to my own diagnosis—they certainly were not in the text. If they were tired after lunch, do something to enliven the class. If they were bored, engage them in a topic like behavioral psychology and conditioning, which was then translated into how to break behavioral habits that they knew they "should" change but, for some reason, couldn't. Each student brought examples of two of these habits to class, and they designed what they might do to change themselves using learning theory and without having to go to a therapist. Talk about capturing their interest.

I fed off them and they off me. I took the pulse of the class through my observations; conversations with them before, during, and after class; and brief assessments, and I adjusted my work based on the data. As success came, I took more risks and they responded. They began to arrive early and stay late with questions and ideas I couldn't have imagined. They even sat closer to the front. At least 10 of these formerly reluctant students made appointments to talk about themselves, and in the course of these conversations, I established allies within the class, along with deep insights about their issues and concerns.

By the end of the course, I had created innumerable designs that woke the class up, made their learning relevant, and kept me from feeling totally incompetent. That was the ultimate win-win. The text didn't matter. What did matter was their intellectual curiosity about things that did. My job was to take the indecipherable language of the text and extract what should, at the very least, be memorable for them. By me becoming a better teacher and facilitator, they became better students. By becoming rigorous with my observations, ideas came. I realized, for instance, that most of the students would rather paint, draw, carve—most anything, really—than sit and read a text of any kind. This led to a discussion of poor study habits and how learning was tied to the ability to internalize information so it was retained over time and retrievable later, whether they liked it or not. That, in turn, led to a series of discussions in class about bad study habits ranging from family of origin issues (again, conditioning) and the role that sleep, drinking, food, and exercise had on the learning process.

I never really understood the turnaround until I critiqued the entire experience with a colleague, along with the hard-earned feedback from my former adversaries, the students. Feedback is, perhaps, the single most valuable tool a facilitator can use and, more than likely, the most threatening. It remains challenging all these years later, because I too want to hear what I want to hear; I want to be liked and appreciated and valued. The result is that self-justification and defensiveness are often close at hand. When I opened myself to the obvious nonverbal feedback available to me and, later, to the information my students were ready to share, I was on the road to becoming a good teacher and better facilitator.

It was my first taste of getting out of my own way, recognizing the negative impact I was creating as a leader, facilitator, and teacher. I was beginning to believe that I as the teacher and facilitator could learn from these totally curious young men and women. It was critical to my further growth—as a person first, and a teacher and facilitator second.

Life or Death in the Jungle

In contrast to his limited understanding of the Tyler art students, this next experience reveals how far Rod had come in understanding intentional facilitation and the creation of well-crafted designs based on a careful, emerging assessment.

This experience is the kind of affirmation we all need to suggest that we are still growing and on track. It was a spontaneous event that I was not prepared to face. Had I not internalized a diagnostic approach and been committed to an intentional way of acting, I would have failed the challenge miserably.

A good friend of mine, George Lakey, is the quintessential advocate for worthy social and political causes. He is a master at confronting perceived hypocrisy and injustice with creative strategies that induce change. You may not believe in all his causes, but you have to respect his combination of personal values, courage, and creativity. An antiwar activist during the Vietnam War, he and a small crew once drove a sampan through the entire Fifth Fleet to bring first aid to wounded North Vietnam troops and civilians. By following his Quaker principles, he confronted a divisive issue with a bold and creative strategy that made a statement and drew the eyes of the world to his efforts. He was antiwar, but mostly, he was attempting to solve, for him, a humanitarian problem. And what were they going to do? Blow the small boat out of the water with the entire world watching? Now that was a "design."

More recently, George was in Thailand, helping to train "human shields"—individuals who voluntarily insert themselves as unarmed neutrals when dealing with two hostile forces, usually prior to a civil war, when citizens are potentially in the crossfire of the two combatants. The shields would move into the breach in an effort to bring the world's attention to the warring parties, with the hope of bringing them to the negotiation table, thus saving human lives. These individuals are not combatants. They strive for dialogue in the midst of high tension. It is hoped that the militants will not shoot or harm them because of the negative press that would result. In this case, the training was in preparation for moving into a Sri Lanka conflict between the rebel Tamil Tigers and the government.

I was brought into George's program to act as a retrospective evaluator of the training course, to be a recorder of the program's history and, perhaps, a source of feedback to my friend and his co-leader once the training was completed. On my arrival, with the training well under way, it became clear that there was a high degree of tension between the leadership and the participant human shields. Not surprisingly, anyone willing to put their life on the line wouldn't hesitate to push back at a leader. In this instance, my friend had miscalculated. He'd not engaged the participants as he would normally have done, and in the absence of this trust, his behavior was perceived as increasingly authoritarian and arrogant. To add fuel to that fire, my friend grew resistant to their feedback. He was, however, even in the midst of his own defensiveness, experienced enough to see that he was losing the confidence of the group, which could jeopardize their training mission. Truth be told, as he'd become older, increasingly honored, and well known as an activist and facilitator, his tolerance for resistance to his ideas had decreased perceptibly. Yet, in other groups, his reputation would carry the day and he would not be faced with the possible rebellion that was mounting in the shields' training camp in Thailand.

While not hired to be a critic of George or of his real-time training, I nevertheless addressed the subject of the group's obvious frustration and resistance. He realized that I had fresh eyes and immediately saw one of his errors. Applying the principles of intentional facilitation and the art of design, I provided my friend with a high-risk but calculated design that shone a light directly on his facilitator role. There, in the middle of the jungle, we took a day out of training for me to interview small clusters of the participants and gather what would be compelling data. He trusted me, and they as well, by the end of that day. The key was when I reported back my boldly honest feedback in a public forum of the entire camp. George knew it wouldn't be pretty.

To some of them, he seemed autocratic and insensitive to their situation. To others, he seemed disconnected from the community, an outsider. But, remarkably, he owned it, first with me, and then with the participants. He'd known he was in trouble and this was the first step essential to reviving his credibility. They knew he had made himself vulnerable and this was his way of apologizing. He knew that he and I were not competing and my intention was to help him and his remarkable program get back on track. Humility is a powerful antidote. And it wasn't a performance to win back the group. He did it because he recognized that he had, on some level, lost his way with this group, and perhaps even more with himself.

Still, it's one thing to hear information from me, and quite another to hear it from the participants, which in this case (and in most cases) needed to be acknowledged through nondefensive responses. So, he agreed to the second part of the design: to take the hour after I presented my findings to give individuals the opportunity to tell him how the situation itself made them feel, from the frustration of the leader's actions to the fears and realities of their training as human shields, how they had lost their sense of empowerment in the community just prior to going to Sri Lanka and putting their lives on the line. It was a chilling, compelling, and heartfelt hour. He listened carefully, nondefensively. And then he responded humbly, admitting he had been insensitive to their process, something he believed in deeply. He did what a truly skilled facilitator would do—took responsibility for his part of the problem.

Clearly, the second part of the design was just as important as the first. Yet, many facilitators would not have had the courage to do what he did—speak from his heart—while being so exposed. His authentic acceptance of his mistakes was the perfect remedy to the mounting negative feelings in the camp. Imagine if most facilitators were willing, on occasion, to admit their failing or some limitation in a public forum? In this instance, some levity was added to the scene because of George's openness.

Facilitation often demands being both humble and vulnerable. This is tricky territory, because people can see, almost instantly, if it's authentic. I knew he could be authentically vulnerable, because he felt so deeply remorseful. Had I not thought he was ready to take that critical step back, the design would have failed. And that is a very different level of diagnosis, one much more challenging than having him only listen to the feelings of the participants.

Such real-time assessment and the willingness to be wrong is, to me, an essential part of facilitation. It takes years of practice, and I'm happy to say that I'm still learning. You can't script it, and you won't see it on any agenda. Yet here is where trust is built, where openness is modeled. While things may not be as dramatic as this for you, there are many opportunities when facilitators can own their mistakes, hear feedback publicly, and then act differently. Some participants later said that because my friend did what he did, he actually gained strength and credibility, and they trusted him much more than when they entered the program based on his reputation. He had earned it.

Courageous Facilitation in the Face of Leadership Denial

As you can see, the role of a facilitator can be broad. There is always the need for a creative event, feedback, or skill in cultivating rich conversations among parties who are reluctant or even antagonistic. Perhaps most important is the facilitator's role as a keen observer and truth teller. It's what has been missing from the following situation for years—at a huge cost.

During the past decade, the Gallup organization has had a huge impact on leadership and the supervisory process. Through a set of simple questions, the organization developed an incisive way to assess a team's or an organization's strengths and limitations in the critical arena of employee satisfaction. They learned that the single most important influence on productivity, turnover, and profits is how the supervisor treats employees, supports them, and shows them that they are important.

One large organization known to pride itself on its family-like culture had its employees—30,000 strong—take the Gallup assessment. The top leadership team was confident the results would place them in the top quartile of comparable companies. To their shocked disbelief, the company was in the lower 30th percentile.

The shock turned to anger. First, the top team blamed Gallup and its instrument. Second, they blamed those reporting to them. A month into the rationalizations and excuses, the president suggested courageously and candidly that the data didn't lie. While he stopped short of taking a hard look at the top team's role in the problem, he helped to stop the finger pointing and blaming. What happened next could have been predicted. He and other leaders pointed down into the still-reeling organization and said to those at the first- and second-line supervisory levels with the lowest scores, "Fix it."

There was no training, no effort to understand the underlying issues that had altered the culture so dramatically over many years, no turning the mirror onto the organization and, more important, onto themselves. The culture of blame—the real problem—was in full bloom.

The unwillingness of the top leaders to own their part of the problem, which is what they modeled, reinforced the climate of secrecy, fear, and denial that permeated all levels of the organization—beginning at the very top. Two years later, expecting large-scale improvement, the assessment was given again. The results, predictably, were worse, because the climate of fear that permeated upward had not changed, and the top leaders had done nothing to change themselves. Success over the years had bred a sense of arrogance and entitlement at the top. Although the company's success continued, the original foundation of trust and openness had diminished. This mistrust was now mirrored in greater turnover, lower morale, and questions about the organization's survivability in an increasingly lean marketplace.

Deteriorating leadership—the movement from collaboration to command and control—had not happened all at once. It had been insidious and cumulative as leaders stopped leading, stopped engaging, stopped being open to criticism and change. The flags and placards on the walls attesting to values of openness and candor had become easily observed hypocrisy that undermined the credibility of leadership. But who would tell them? The cost to morale, company loyalty, and productivity is hard to estimate—but it was more than management was willing to own. Imagine the impact this had every time there was a meeting, every time a serious problem had to be solved. And imagine the influence this had on any facilitator attempting to open such a meeting to a more honest, direct, and open conversation, where the goal would be to ensure greater truth telling and real collaboration. But if not a courageous facilitator, then whom?

As with many organizations, the downturn of 2008 forced some deep, often searing introspection at the top of this and many organizations. Within this organization, some restructuring, an effort at introspection, and a few mergers created some of the changes essential to winning back part of the lost trust. It had taken decades for the company to become inured to its leadership failures, and it would take several years to regain employees' trust and confidence, which they had once taken for granted. But although the jury is still out, the trend is positive.

An acknowledged fear is that buying other organizations will be a temporary fix to the issues of trust and morale. More essential is that trust and candor among the senior leadership team is restored first, which can then flow down into the larger organization. That will require a further owning of problems and modeling of changes in visible ways. As with most challenging situations, it begins with the top team and demands the design mentality discussed in the rest of this book. Facilitators often find themselves in a catalyst role, where they can open the door to new designs that are meant to encourage greater candor, feedback, and honesty, while at the same time protecting members who still carry fear from years of intimidation and conflict avoidance. But a culture where criticism does not move upward demands facilitators who can risk the consequence of telling the truth and are encouraged to do so by those at the top.

The following chapters contain considerations for facilitators and their organizations who are ready to expand both the facilitator role and the array of choices open to them as they creatively seek new approaches to traditional activities.

3

CREATIVITY, STRUCTURE, AND DESIGN

Regardless of how distasteful most meetings are, we live increasingly in a world full of them: one on one, four, eight, 20, or more. Every day we run from one to the next, breathless, frequently feeling ill-prepared as a member or leader. A meeting is where we are led, informed, criticized, and delegated to. It is the place where most traditional leadership occurs—at least in terms of strategy execution. And unfortunately, it's where participants often feel disengaged, uninvolved, and impotent. Facilitators have more opportunity than most others to change the often-unsettling equation. But, they too frequently settle for mediocrity, not willing to risk the creative act that might breathe both meaning and life into same old, same old.

We are painting a boldly unflattering picture of most meetings only because it is true. They have become the bane of leaders and participants alike and can wear negatively on both productivity and morale—the cultural psyche of teams and organizations. After all, when was the last time you felt disappointed that a meeting was canceled?

The art of design is meant to provide new skills and ways of doing things that will turn the tide. This often depends, of course, on facilitators' willingness to lead, to take a risk and challenge themselves.

Oh, come on, you say. Typically, as the facilitator, you have a limited amount of time, an agenda or set of agendas (some hidden), and a group of people who just want you to get on with it so they can rush off to their next meeting. There is little time for niceties, and besides, most people's heads are still in their last meeting or in the important one that lies ahead. Now, make something meaningful out of that.

And as for the beleaguered leader whose meeting it theoretically is, there has been little time to design anything, so they unceremoniously hand the responsibility to you, the facilitator, with little real authority and the goal of getting on with it, whatever that may mean. So, without a high bar to drive your own interest, you cobble together an agenda (probably not getting it out to the participants in advance) and you begin with the mantra borrowed from most leaders: "Well, we have a lot to cover and not much time, so let's start." The air is somber at best or resentful at worst. You begin.

Consider this: Any time you have the audacity to call a meeting to take people's time and energy, it's an opportunity to bring a modicum of success into the participants' day. You either make something positive of the opportunity, or you don't. Are you willing to embody that? Most are not, and they will make excuses that the outcome of the meeting is supposedly out of their control. But, here are no excuses. What you do as facilitator is defined as your leadership.

Having a Diagnostic Mentality

As a facilitator with a diagnostic mentality, whenever you walk into a room, ask yourself, "What's needed? What value can I add? How can I contribute to the goals—either task or process?" It doesn't matter if you're in charge. What matters is that you are continually assessing the needs as they change. It's a very opportunistic attitude with the assumption that if you can help, you will. You are always assessing the possibilities. And, when you leave, you have to ask, "How could I have contributed more, and why didn't I?" That's why you call yourself a facilitator.

It is an attitude that you carry wherever you are in the world. It's active, not passive. It is the expectation of providing service to the group whenever the opportunity avails itself. It is driven by an ongoing assessment of the ever-changing reality of a given business or plan—not by ego. It's an assumption that says you are an active player in the game whether labeled that or not; that you have certain skills and behaviors that may be helpful, whether acknowledged by anyone or not. Thus, it is your knowing and preparedness that changes your role from the beginning, and you will be wary of who has the real authority and their ego invested in what's happening. But, if you can be of value, that should always be your intention.

Now, shifting to a meeting (one on one, three or four, a team meeting, or other gatherings) where you have responsibility for accomplishing work, it is up to you to know the climate of the group, the expected deliverables now and later, where potential trouble lies that might sabotage success, and what level of contribution is needed. And ultimately, this includes what the other participants think about the outcomes that result and how much they might want to engage in the process.

All this is woven into a consideration of the time available. There are other more pointed questions that will be considered, but for now, it is this attitude that is foundational for everything that follows.

Consider this definition of meeting design: Using diagnostic information to develop activities to help a group or organization systematically move toward the completion of both task and process goals. With this in mind, the design and structure of a meeting can have a huge influence on its potential success. Facilitators can often control planned meeting activities, the location, the layout, and timing, all of which will influence the outcomes. For example, it is not wise to jump into the most contentious, urgent, or critical part of an agenda first thing in a meeting, as participants need time to get psychologically present and settle in. Facilitators need to understand the urgency of the tasks and adjust their approach by continuously asking, "What are the initial needs of the group?" Are they serving their own needs or that of the group? For many, this kind of rigorous questioning is seen as a bother rather than a critical aspect of any gathering.

This chapter describes how creative meeting design and choices relating to meeting structure can greatly contribute to successful outcomes.

The Task and Process Equation

As discussed in chapter 1, you can think of every meeting as a balance between task goals and process goals (Figure 3-1). The task goals—the "what" of work (measured deliverables) is commonly the exclusive focus of meetings. Yet, how the work is accomplished and how people feel both during and after the experience can have a significant impact on the team or organization involved. How facilitators treat the participants can leave them feeling either engaged and energized or frustrated and depleted, and this has nothing to do with the "what" or the goals of the meeting itself. Additionally, your attitude will influence your willingness to take action and participate in the necessary follow-up, homework, or commitments that will directly influence the next meeting.

Figure 3-1. Every Meeting Has Task and Process Goals

Facilitators are often much more comfortable dealing with the task side of this equation, because it is easier to define and more comfortable than dealing with the process side. For example, a team of leaders has 40 minutes on an agenda to make a marketing decision. What to do is a no-brainer. With limited time and a specific decision to be made, the facilitator does what is almost always done: goes around the table hearing from each member, and then looks to the leader to make the decision. And, because it is likely that the decision has been debated by key leaders prior to the meeting, the discussion is simply a means of making the participants feel included. There is no time for a penetrating discussion among all those present.

However, most morale problems stem from indiscretions in the "how" domain of process rather than the "what" domain of the task. The "how" side deals with how the work of the task is going to be accomplished. It includes how people will be involved, how the facilitator wants them to feel as participants, what kind of emotional baggage everyone brings to the group, and what needs addressing if the task is to be successfully completed. In the previous example, there is little interest in the process. Everyone just wants to complete the task and get it off the agenda. Habit runs the meeting's process rather than a more creative and interesting process worthy of the decision that is about to be made.

Think about the tensions in your own team or organization. Do you think they stem from the task side of this balance, or the process side?

Thus, to produce a well-crafted meeting design, facilitators need to first identify both the task and process goals. Doing this will ensure that they are prompted to consider which designs are required to achieve all the goals—not just the task ones. The result will be increased productivity in achieving the task and increased morale due to the process the participants used to get there. It's not that a good outcome cannot be produced without considering how morale is being influenced. However, if morale is not actively considered, there is a good chance that dysfunctional norms such as talking over others, interrupting, and not listening will become part of the process. We are usually in too much of a hurry to address these kinds of process issues when they occur, and they are rarely discussed at the end of a session, when everyone is eager to leave. By not addressing these insensitive behaviors that turn a group off, they are actually reinforced. This is further exacerbated in many cases because the norms of the team or organization reflect aversion and denial of most conflict. Speaking the truth about process is bound to raise some ire because somebody has dropped the ball.

Along with being mindful of both task and process goals, other design considerations include whether to stand or sit; use PowerPoint, multimedia tools, or a flip chart; and whether to speak with objectivity or with passion in attempting to sell a point. All these make a difference. Similarly, providing materials in advance, breaking the team into large or small groups, the time of day, the physical setting of the room, and the facilitator's dress, tone of voice, eye contact, and use of humor can all influence success. The devil is most certainly in these details.

As the complexity of the meeting or project increases, so does the complexity of the variables that need to be considered. For example, a systemwide change initiative would also involve factors such as the history of previous changes, the political realities that exist, the powerful cliques that drive most solutions, the triggers that may create dissent, the strength and attitudes within various silos, and the trust that exists throughout the organization. The facilitator also needs to know if there is any unfinished business needing to be addressed before progress can be made on a larger initiative. Again, it's all in the details. If the facilitator does not have this detailed knowledge of the group or organization, they, and ultimately the participants, will be limited in what they can accomplish. It also demands courage, skill, and patience to address the underlying factors that can influence success. For facilitators, as in the case of the human shields, it is often easier to remain in the backwaters of denial and avoidance than to rock the proverbial boat with unvarnished truth.

Breaking Down an Example of a Complex Design

The following is an example of some of the thinking that goes into meeting structure and design. The need in this particular case is for a meeting to decide which of three virtual learning providers will be selected to produce custom content for a company's e-learning suite. The key stakeholders who are to attend the meeting have been identified by the meeting sponsor, who has engaged us to facilitate the discussion on their behalf. We have been given one hour to achieve the final decision on provider selection—that all stakeholders are expected to buy into

(Figure 3-2). While the task is challenging, we believe it's manageable if we are rigorous with our process, using a design that reflects crucial aspects of both task and process goals and the consequences of each.

Figure 3-2. Sample Meeting Factors

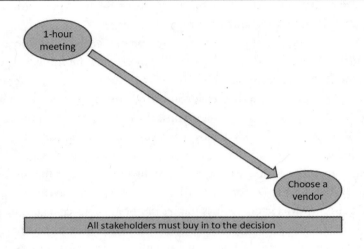

The first thing to think about is the amount of knowledge that the stakeholders will need to have prior to walking into the meeting. We have only 60 minutes, so this means that there will be no time for the stakeholders to review the detailed bids during the meeting. This leads us to the first process goal: Provide the participants with detailed knowledge of the three bids beforehand (Figure 3-3). The problem, of course, will be motivating them to read and understand the materials. Meeting success can be diminished when only half the group has completed the assignment. Thus, the players must know what is expected of them coming into the meeting.

The second process goal—ensure 100 percent buy-in—comes from the sponsor's direction that all stakeholders must buy into the ultimate decision. This will need to be reflected in every piece of the meeting design, starting with the circulation of the bids before the meeting. These will be provided via a pre-read, to be circulated one week ahead of the scheduled meeting time. We will also give the stakeholders a chance to ask any questions they might have concerning the pre-read before attending the session.

Figure 3-3. First Process Goal

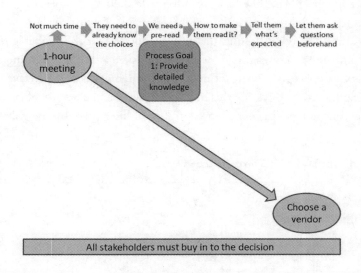

Prompting for questions can have several functions: It makes sure participants know the reading is required, it gives them a chance to digest the content, and it makes sure nobody is holding questions until the meeting. Don't just assume that people will ask questions, because they probably won't. Create the expectation of questions by setting up a brief call with each stakeholder, or a conference call in which each stakeholder has five minutes to present their questions. By getting questions out beforehand, we can avoid wasting time with them in the meeting. It's this kind of detail that can undermine the meeting's success if it's not planned for.

The next consideration is the third process goal: Decide how to decide at the start of the meeting by spending a few minutes facilitating this decision. Without this structure, there will not be time during the 60-minute meeting to decide how to decide. Failure to do so can sabotage the entire effort. For every participant to buy into the final decision, it is best to let them have input into how the decision will be made—and to do this before the decision actually needs to be made. An open discussion will probably not work unless the participants are well versed in different decision-making methods and their strengths and limitations. As the facilitator, providing two suitable choices would be a good option; then, let the group vote on a two-thirds or majority vote to decide. People like having a choice.

Setting the meeting up in this way is also serving process goal 2—both letting the group feel ownership of the meeting process and giving them a quick win right off the bat (Figure 3-4). They have already made their first, albeit easy, decision. Waiting to decide how to decide until the moment of truth can lead to manipulation and resistance by those in the group who see that the probable outcome will go against them. For example, people could force a discussion to increase the two-thirds vote to, say, a 75 percent majority requirement if they perceive the vote as not going their way. By doing this in advance, we can cast a sense of inevitability that the participants will generally accept. They'll likely play by the rules they've agreed to.

Figure 3-4. Second and Third Process Goals

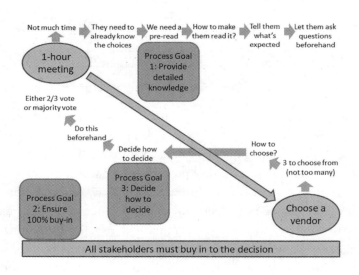

The next challenge is the fourth process goal: Develop the criteria used to determine the best decision (Figure 3-5). In this case, we need to design a meeting process for achieving this goal that will be explained to the group. Some example criteria might be cost to deliver the custom content, time to develop it, how intuitive the user interface is, or the quality of styling and graphics. This helps remove some irrational thinking from the discussion and from the ultimate decision.

Figure 3-5. Fourth Process Goal

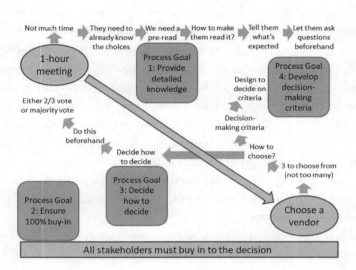

An option for the design would be to divide the group into pairs or threes (depending on the group size), with each subgroup developing a list of their top five criteria, in order of importance. We will need to do the math so that we end up with four even subgroups.

We'll give the subgroups 10 minutes to construct their lists, and tell them that they can present only criteria that every member agrees to. This might mean some subgroups may have only two or three criteria—perfectly acceptable. These instructions will result in people being able to agree more easily. Our experience is that people are more willing to compromise when their voice in the final decision making will be lost if they don't. Most subgroups get stuck when individual egos get in the way and consequently they have no way of influencing the final decision.

Following this, we'll combine the four subgroups into two larger groups, and give these two new groups 10 minutes to negotiate a combined prioritized list of their top five to seven criteria. It is likely that there will already some overlap within the various subgroups. If not, they still need to agree, if they wish to influence the final vote.

Finally, both half-groups will come together and share their ideas. Inevitably there will again be some overlap between the two groups as they look to find the five to seven best criteria. If the two half-groups generate only four agreed-upon criteria between them, we'll give them another 10 minutes to agree on any additional criteria.

This design will both satisfy process goal 4 and contribute to process goal 2 by rapidly building consensus among the group on what is important, without having to lobby for any particular solution. By using clear rules to govern discussion and structuring time, success is almost guaranteed. Called collapsing consensus, the design assumes that such consensus building is a negotiation, and most individuals will be able to live with the final list of criteria. Done well, this aspect of the overall design will make the final selection of the provider considerably easier. Leaving the process open without such designed structure invites the chaotic, ego-driven discussion that we often experience, with many individuals becoming passive and a few (usually the same) individuals dominating the discussion and the eventual decision. That approach is certainly easier for the facilitator and ensures the kind of dysfunction we so often experience.

Finally, the task goal is this: Choose a provider (Figure 3-6). Instead of facilitating a contentious and unstructured discussion, we'll employ a very rigorous process of scoring each bid against the prioritized criteria, then use the method identified in process goal 3 (two-thirds or majority vote) to settle any

Figure 3-6. The Task Goal

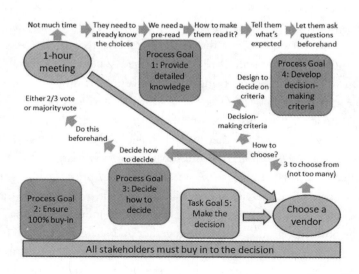

ties. Imagine how easy the decision making will be using this meeting design, versus a more traditional approach of going around the table and having a few powerful individuals dominate the discussion and the eventual decision. In this example, participants could decide in 10 minutes because using weighted criteria makes it easy to determine the best choice. In another scenario, egos would likely rule.

You may have noticed that there are four process goals and only one task goal in this particular meeting design (Figure 3-7). You might imagine that so much focus on the process would extend the time spent on the design. Not so; structure and the carefully monitored use of time results in a product that would take longer with a more open and unfettered process.

Figure 3-7. Four Process Goals, One Task Goal

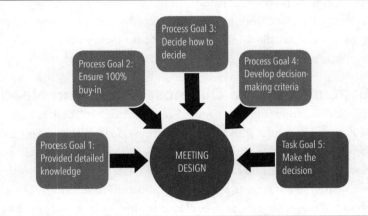

Design as a Creative Act

Designing meetings to move a team or system forward is definitely a creative act. There are no boilerplates, no predesigned formulas for what to do, no one-size-fits-all approach for meeting types. Instead, facilitators must ask themselves, "What can I create that will benefit this group, overcome resistance, or accelerate the work these people do as a team?" Choosing which of the designs in your toolbox to use in any given moment, deciding which combinations would work well together, or modifying the tools to better suit a particular situation are all creative acts. Our effort here is to provide additional ideas to expand your thinking while you read this book.

You can also use creative thinking when holding a single meeting with multiple agenda items. Each agenda item can be thought of as a mini meeting, having a beginning, a middle, and an end, in addition to having both task and process goals. The only limits to the creative process are in your mind. Asking questions concerning time availability, desired engagement levels, and task and process goals can improve both participant satisfaction and the quality of the eventual outcomes. Will this approach by the facilitator require more planning time and creative thinking? Yes. And the result will be greater productivity and satisfaction at the end.

It helps to have a design buddy, someone who can help you think about your designs in a diagnostic way—offering "what if?" questions or testing your design assumptions. This is not always possible, so we have developed the following 15 diagnostic questions that help facilitators decide on the nature and flow of their activities, the kinds of involvement desired, and the layout of the room. All are important creative considerations to achieve the greatest success. These can provide facilitators with a certain rigor often not present by the owner of the particular meeting or event.

Essential Questions to Diagnose the Group Need

Breaking bad habits or adding new, more positive actions to the facilitator repertoire usually requires practice with lots of repetition, along with a deep belief that the new behavior is a better replacement for old actions. When at all possible, facilitators need to practice the new behavior in a safe environment so they can actually experience the advantages. Our use of animation in the videos that accompany this book is meant to provide confidence in this process. Still, the following 15 questions are intended to be foundational for any design the facilitator should want to experience. Some of these are similar to a pilot's checklist; others may seem like the task or process thinking we touched on before. Still, they are present in any good design.

Are the task- or outcome-based goals clear, well articulated, and agreed to by those participating? Is the meeting itself necessary?
It is extraordinary how rarely these commonsense conditions are all present and how often the meeting adds little value. People often act out of habit, and many meetings are, in fact, acts of habit and unnecessary. Having the courage not to have a meeting can test your mettle.

Do the agenda items reflect the goals? Is there sufficient time and resources to accomplish them?

Stuffing 10 pounds of agenda into a five-pound meeting reflects a lack of rigor and destroys any possibility for creative design work. It also leaves everyone feeling frustrated. This is the reality of many meetings and their resulting dysfunction. It takes courage to undertake only goals that have been thoroughly scrutinized and aligned realistically with the time and resources available.

Is the process aspect of the meeting addressed—how the task or work is to be accomplished—with attention to how people are involved and how they feel about what is happening?

This is where morale and productivity intersect. If people are really engaged in the process, the outcome will be much more powerful and success more easily achieved.

Are the right people present to accomplish these goals? Do they have everything they need?

How often are the necessary resources absent? How often do people attend who add no value to the meeting? Having only those people present who add value is another act of discipline and courage. Once in attendance, it is up to the facilitator not to waste their precious time. That is the primary facilitator function.

For each task or agenda item, is there a creatively designed activity that meets the unique need of the moment?

This assumes the facilitator, prior to the meeting, has set aside critical planning time to create appropriately designed strategies that will address the needs of the group. Doing this with another person is a good way to test assumptions and to build design skills throughout the organization. Like we said, each separate agenda item is a mini meeting. Such understanding reflects a true comprehension of design.

What level of involvement is needed from those present to make certain that the best ideas are shared and the resources in the room are fully utilized?

Full engagement by all the participants is one of the key variables that people don't always consider. Too often the same few individuals dominate the discussion, causing passivity, resentment, and dependency among the rest. Not everything has to be shared, but, when feasible, what is the level of collaboration that needs to occur in relation to each issue or agenda item? Having "ownership" of the various outcomes is key to the overall success of the meeting.

Is decision making a critical component of the meeting? Is it clear how the decision is going to be made in advance of the decision itself?

Decision making should be a carefully designed part of any problem-solving process, not a reaction or afterthought. Who has the real authority? Is that clear? Can everybody agree to the method that will be used to make the decision? These are key ingredients of trust, and they must be established prior to the point of the decision to head off manipulation in the group. Decisions are at the heart of understanding where power and authority really lie. It is a source of much discontent.

Is there any "unfinished business" that could sabotage the desired behavior or group effectiveness?

Unresolved conflicts among participants, and the unwillingness to tackle them, can damage any meeting. It's the facilitator's responsibility to ensure that these factors do not undermine the desired outcomes. This may require pre-meeting work or some intervention in the session itself, built into the time available. Here again is where the facilitator has to lead from intention and courage. Your alignment with the actual leader of the session is crucial prior to the meeting itself.

Has the facilitator thoughtfully considered time?

Time can have a huge impact on outcomes. The time of day or the day of the week can determine levels of energy and motivation. The time available is a critical issue in any planning. And the amount of time can be used as a tool to increase meeting efficiencies. For example, having participants work on specific tasks in subgroups, and giving them 10 minutes rather than 20 or 30, can help. Or telling the group that you want three ideas or whatever number they can agree on in the time available. It's amazing how these kinds of ground rules can help small groups move toward consensus. People rarely question the amount of time given for an activity, and generally they will use all the time allotted. You can even create a sense of urgency where there is none by making the group work under a time crunch. Using time creatively is a critical element in the design process. The goal is not to increase anxiety through unnecessary urgency. Rather, it is using time as a critical resource and helping the participants understand why you are using it that way as you move forward. Such brief explanations can be motivating and help participants begin thinking about how they use time in their own meetings.

Has an effort been made to assess the potential consequences that could affect success? Have assumptions been tested?

Facilitators, like everyone else, can get lazy, becoming inattentive or simply ignoring the limitations of any given design. That people see what they want to see can be a hard-won truth. Therefore, asking yourself, "What could go wrong?" is a critical question in any design activity. Similarly, have the assumptions—realistic statements of the "givens" or variables mentioned previously—that are driving the meeting been clarified and addressed in advance of the meeting? Lastly, what do people need to know in advance if success is to be assured?

Does the design feel routine rather than creative?

Often it is an unwillingness to challenge and think outside the box that can result in participants not feeling stimulated or engaged. Most people actually love doing out of the ordinary things as long as they make sense. Even previously successful designs can become old rapidly. Boredom, in turn, can spawn passivity, disengagement, and inaction. We've found that a design like Future Search (see chapter 5) can be overused because it works. And the result is that over time, participants are less enthused. The key is to create the "best" design called for in the current situation.

Is physical space utilized to maximize participation?

How often do facilitators become victims of the space used for a meeting? The space can determine what occurs. For example, a large table can dictate where people sit and how they interact with one another—or not. Predictable seating by members of a team or committee can reflect power in the group and who gets heard. It's also easy to see how a classroom with chairs in rows leads to less involvement and more of the teacher "talking at" those present. Open seating, on the other hand, can result in the flexible use of small groups. It's amazing how easy it is to turn participants off simply by how the room is structured. The combination of space and time can have a remarkable influence on the energy and vitality of those in the room. Ten people sitting around a table is often the norm that results in predictable patterns of who talks and who gets heard. It can be the death knell for meaningful conversation. We have created a wide range of designs that address how to stimulate meaningful conversation.

Are difficult people allowed to interfere with the desired outcome because of their negative or damaging behavior?

It is the facilitator's job to confront people or actions that diminish or undermine the group. Heading these problems (often from the same offenders) off at the pass can save a meeting from being derailed. Avoiding handling these individuals only reinforces their undesirable behavior. If it is your meeting, you must act like it; set ground rules to avoid the dysfunctional behavior that can hamper the group's effectiveness, and gain the offenders' support. Often this needs to occur before the meeting, so you do not have to stop the meeting and change course or deal directly with the individuals. You don't have to use threats, but a no-nonsense attitude is essential, as well as the courage to act when necessary.

Something as simple as putting two talkative people in the same subgroup of two or three people can result in more opportunities for others to be heard. There are many creative configurations of group members that can be used within any meeting. To have a meeting hijacked falls on the shoulders of the facilitator, because they should have seen it coming or had a plan B in mind to deal with it.

Are summaries of progress made and follow-up commitments formalized? Is accountability clearly established prior to people leaving? Are promises kept?

We've found a lack of rigor to be the single largest reason for disillusionment among both facilitators and participants. The consequence? Passivity and noninvolvement in the future. The facilitator needs to ensure meaningful accountability and compliance, with agreed-upon commitments and consequences. Lack of follow-up is a morale buster and needs to be addressed in the group, with clear ground rules and infractions openly discussed among the participants. For people not to do what they have agreed to will lessen the value of any meeting and the commitment of members in the future.

Is every meeting of an hour or more evaluated in light of what worked or didn't work? What could be done to improve the outcome the next time?

Done well, this is the best antidote to bad meetings and failed initiatives. It requires courageous facilitators who demand this level of accountability for themselves and those attending. Corrective action and follow-up will break habitual and boring meetings of virtually every kind, but that starts with you having the will to stop the train and look hard at your successes and failures. Such modeling can set a precedent for future meetings and increase trust and the willingness to experiment.

These questions may not all be asked every time, but it is easy to see the value of using them when they are appropriate. Once again, it's like a pilot going down a checklist before takeoff—after a while, the checks become second nature. Anybody can learn them, and the answers provide the diagnostic mindset essential in determining the nature of the design(s) that will be created. Facilitators, skilled in the use of these questions, will immediately open themselves to many new choices for creating challenging, motivating, and engaging meetings.

This chapter is intended to whet your appetite for what lies ahead. Now, equipped with a diagnostic lens and a deeper understanding of the task and process dimensions of any meeting or agenda item, you are armed with many more choices for improving your own effectiveness as a facilitator.

The next chapters are deeper probes into all aspects of design and the discipline that can drive you toward more creative activities that not only increase effective participation, but also reflect a better use of time and resources. By the time we reach the second part of the book, you will be ready to observe an array of classic designs, and the accompanying videos will increase your confidence in using them. It will be as though you're sitting next to the participants.

Even more important, you will have the assurance to create your own designs as you draw from the diagnostic questions reviewed here and the kinds of activities demonstrated by our avatars. You will never settle for same old, same old again.

4

FACILITATION FOR ORGANIZATIONS AND TEAMS

Want to be a facilitator in today's world? Get ready for a lifelong challenge. It begins with a willingness to look at yourself, the impact you have on others, and how you get in your own way. From there it moves to understanding those you have the nerve to lead. And, finally, it turns to internalizing the tools and skills essential for being successful in a demanding world. Sergeant Hatchel's tough-minded view of what it took to be a marine evolved from his firsthand experience observing men dying because they weren't prepared. His intentions were absolutely clear, as must yours be.

First, the intention. Then, the strategy to achieve that intention. With dedication and practice, the strategy becomes the art of design.

Transforming facilitation into a creative act that's supported by strategically placed designs is the goal of this book. It requires a flexible, creative, adaptable individual, with a diagnostic mentality and the courage to act on ideas when needed. The intentional facilitator continually asks this question: Do the behaviors I am exhibiting lead to the outcomes I intend, whether in measured deliverables or in how people feel about themselves and one another? This is true whether in real time or further in the future. The answer—if yes—reflects the blending of both the task and process aspects of the work equation.

Incorporating Creative Facilitation Into Everyday Meetings

At the same time, many facilitators have lost their understanding of how to motivate the adult learners they face every day. Thus, as we discuss the concept of strategic design as an art, it will be helpful to reintroduce ourselves to what motivates people to care and engage in whatever it is we are attempting to do.

Here are four things that you should be conscious of regarding meetings in general. Had Rod known these while at the Tyler Art School, he would have been able to save himself and others considerable pain:

1. Unless a speaker is extraordinarily charismatic or knowledgeable, or talking about something of serious interest, the average person rapidly loses the ability to remember critical content after only 15 to 20 minutes of listening. Most information shared after 30 minutes cannot be recalled a week later. So, what does that say about all those unbearably boring and long-winded information sessions and PowerPoint presentations people are required to attend? A facilitator's job is to connect with their audience and, in the process, energize them and tap into their latent curiosity.

2. Many people are easily bored in a world of increasing sound bites and huge amounts are often predictable, a sure avenue to inattention. It's your job to stimulate, challenge, and excite—to capture their interest. Relevance and participation are certain antidotes to boredom—but these are relatively rare meeting characteristics.

3. In many meetings, individuals are distracted by the memory of events that are causing them stress, anxiety, frustration, or anger—preoccupations that flavor what is heard or not heard. Unless something can grab their interest and involve them psychologically or emotionally, attention and retention will be sorely tested. Further, when learning is personal, it's much easier to retain the information.

4. Meetings can be breeding grounds for fear. There is fear of who is present and how their image may be affected by any error or impropriety on their part. There is fear of what is being said and its potential implications for them. The result is an increasing aversion to

conflict or potential conflict, that, in turn, influences what people are willing to say and to whom they are willing to say it. This results in a less-than-authentic meeting with few risks being taken by those present.

For many, meetings represent a minefield of uncontrollable variables. No wonder the same two or three people continue to dominate a typical meeting while the others sit back contributing little or nothing. So, all that said, whose responsibility is it to create an interesting, meaningful, engaging, and productive meeting of any kind?

Our 13 classic designs in part II of this book will demonstrate wide-ranging ideas of how to engage people in relation to many kinds of agendas. But even more important is that by reading these designs carefully, it will ignite your own ideas about how to better utilize the people in the room, how to manage time more creatively, and how even the smallest changes can bring new meaning and enthusiasm into any meeting.

The Dilemma of a Facilitator's Good Intentions

"Having good intentions" means you tried or you didn't mean to do what you did. Or, you're really better than you performed, so don't get mad because you screwed up. Consequently, "good intentions" becomes an excuse or an easy way out of accountability.

Intentional facilitation is very different; it has a much more powerful nuance. Here, intention is wrapped into a commitment to act in a certain way, no matter what. It means that you have assessed what is needed and will act on that assessment with a personal pledge to do what is essential and to tough it out regardless of the consequences, unless the need changes. Sergeant Hatchel would have said that in most cases, there are simply no excuses, no blaming others. It was your decision and your behavior to own. The same thing can be said of many facilitators who are unwilling to step up and provide the absolute best design possible, and then evaluate its effectiveness given the task and process goals that have been created.

But this is not a marine talking; rather, it is any facilitator who is committed to doing the right thing in any moment. It's a disciplined, rigorous attitude that colors everything you do when in such a role. It's not something to be used once in a while. It assumes that every action you take as a facilitator depends on asking the following questions:

- What is my goal; what is my intention to act in this moment?
- What is the outcome that I desire?

- What do I want those participating to experience during the process?
- How do I want them to feel at the end of the experience, when we are finished and they are walking out the door talking about it?
- What do I want them to remember?
- If I didn't achieve the outcome, why not, and what could I have done differently to have made things better?

As a facilitator, these are the rigorous questions to which I hold myself accountable. And whom do I blame if my intentions aren't successful? No one. Again, it rests with me. Even if I'm unable to control everything completely, I most likely can determine the possibility of failure and should have factored it in. It quite simply means owning up to both success and failure—assessing success so it can be replicated, and failure to prevent its reoccurrence. Can we learn from failure? Absolutely. Should effort be praised? Yes.

In fearful workplaces that are increasingly conflict- and risk-averse, excuses and blame are all too often assigned to others. We fear being isolated and shamed by our mistakes and by bosses who won't forget. Consequently, we draw others in to share our fear and pain and, paradoxically, create a pool of mutual blame, hoping to reduce the potential of serious personal repercussions.

Intentionality stops the cycle of blame, shame, fear, and caution that permeates many teams and organizations. And, as you can tell by now, such intention requires work and commitment. How refreshing it is to hear individuals take responsibility for their mistakes or dysfunctions! And these are not gratuitous statements hoping others will say, "Oh no, Rod, it wasn't your fault." No, these are heartfelt statements that reflect what went wrong and what they learned from it.

The Facilitator's Behavior Quiz

Facilitation has always been about getting the essential things done—and influencing others to do what you want or need them to do. It really is that simple, and much of this longstanding idea has been carried into the complexities of modern life. But, as usual, the devil is in the details.

We've been conducting evaluations of facilitators for 30 years and aligning the results with the most current research. At this point, we'd like you to test yourself as a facilitator against the following behavioral criteria we have culled from work experiences in a hundred organizations. We believe they are essential in today's complex world. The statements enable us to measure the behaviors that result in great facilitation—the ultimate goal of any facilitator.

The 10 statements are in a relative order of importance with the assumption that you need some in order to use others. All are essential and the absence of even one will diminish your effectiveness. Are there others? For sure. But this is a manageable list and will, hopefully, challenge some of your assumptions as you see how each relates to the others and, in turn, how they relate to you.

So, evaluate yourself in relation to the 10 statements that describe your efforts at facilitation. Use a seven-point scale, with 7 representing absolute effectiveness, 4 moderate effectiveness, and 2 very limited effectiveness. As a self-diagnostic, it will help reveal where you need to focus as you increase your ability to be intentional and design effectively.

Some would say that the 10 behavioral skills laid out here are too many; they create unreasonable expectations for already busy facilitators. We believe that they are absolutely fundamental. What they aren't, for most of us, is internalized. They suggest the right way of doing business: all the time.

It takes courage to undertake a tough-minded self-assessment. Most people know who they are as facilitators—their inherent strengths and areas of needed development, or those things that hold them back. We may not like saying them out loud, but we know. Well done to those of you who will actually answer these tough questions honestly, and use the results to increase your effectiveness as a facilitator.

To lack any of these qualities in your behavioral repertoire will limit you. Therefore, having an awareness of your current skill level is an essential first step. Once you have a true understanding of how to craft designs to ensure the fulfillment of each of these standards, your capacity to facilitate will increase dramatically. Most of us depend on a few, habitual responses that make us predictable, perhaps lacking in creativity or in the ability to meet the changing needs of the team in any given moment. Yet, with a bit of investment each of these skills is within your grasp.

Finally, there is no expectation that every facilitator should be perfect in their execution. It takes time to break old habits and let go of behaviors that diminish our effectiveness. And of course, there are other skills we could easily add to our list. But these are a good beginning. They might also determine whether you wish to stop reading now, because it won't get easier! That's not a threat, just the reality that habits and perceptions are hard to break. While the focus of this book is on both the how and the what of design, many of the value-based skills and behaviors identified here support the notions of intentionality and the art of design. The 13 designs that will be provided later correlate directly to almost all these value-based, behaviorally defined statements. Use the boxes provided to record your scores. Remember: 7 = absolute effectiveness; 4 = moderate; 2 = very limited effectiveness.

1. Your ability to develop a set of "lived" core values that your team members are committed to live by.

Many teams and organizations have core values, and all too often they become placards on the wall, with little relationship between what members say and what they actually do. To say, "We value collaboration," for example, and then not to build collaboration into the management process is a sure avenue to low morale and passive employees. Successful core values (often no more than four to six) need to be observable and measurable, with both individuals and teams accountable to living them and real consequences for those unwilling to abide by them. For high-performing teams, values are the foundation upon which everything else is built. Be respectful, demonstrate integrity, be supportive of one another, and provide feedback in everything we do are just a few examples. They provide a road map for facilitators and the individuals with whom they work.

2. Your ability and willingness to demonstrate listening, and to communicate clearly what you have heard.

Active listening is a key ingredient in respecting others and building trust. It represents a clearly observable and measurable behavior that, almost universally, is easy to recognize. It is, for many, the first building block of any solid relationship.

3. Your ability to collaborate with those you lead—to engage them in issues important to them so they feel ownership in decisions and strategies that influence their experience in the team or organization.

Research shows a positive relationship between morale, productivity, and the degree people feel empowered to influence the ideas and decisions that affect them. Soliciting ideas and solutions from group or team members is a sign of respect.

4. Your ability to provide goals that capture the interest of team or organizational members, including goals for a compelling vision.

People who come to work every day want to be inspired, to feel that they make a difference. One of the powerful means of building team cohesion is having team members committed to goals that make a difference—regardless of whether they're task or process goals. "Owning" such goals as employees and participants becomes a powerful motivator, especially when the achievement of the outcomes is visible and acknowledged.

5. Your ability and willingness to provide skillful feedback to individuals, teams, and, when necessary, leaders of the team or organization. [ ]
Feedback could easily be seen as the single most valuable skill a facilitator can have. Done well, it can help improve individual performance, alter goals, and direct changes essential to the individual, team, or organization. Done ineffectively, it can alienate and marginalize individuals. In relation to team performance, it is the litmus test that best differentiates high-performing teams from mediocre ones. Here is an area that touches every aspect of management and leadership. Yet, in conflict-averse organizations, it can be a huge problem, because mistrust will drive feedback underground.

6. Your openness and willingness to solicit feedback and, when appropriate, use it. [ ]
A certain way that facilitators alienate themselves from others is to have feedback going in only one direction—from the more powerful to the less powerful. Effective feedback can influence every level of team and organizational life. It needs to be two-way. Facilitators must be willing to model skills in both giving and receiving feedback. Many top-down, command and control organizations do not create the climate of trust that is so essential if feedback is to be useful.

7. Your ability and willingness to solve complex issues, especially with those who are affected. [ ]
One of the often-used definitions of a facilitator is somebody who is skilled in the art of problem solving. The problem is that most facilitators have a very narrowly defined repertoire of problem-solving strategies and experiences. Yet, there are hundreds of kinds of problems that demand widely differing problem-solving strategies. Each strategy can be perceived as a design—hopefully chosen based on a sensitive diagnosis of the needs of the individual or group and dependent on who is involved, historic realities, and whether decisions have to be made.

8. Your ability to provide individuals with an honest and direct performance appraisal process that focuses on measured accountability and the subsequent development of those being assessed. [ ]

In recent years, measuring individual performance has become increasingly ineffective as roles and tasks have become more narrowly defined and personal development of less interest. The challenges of performance management and supervisory relationships are further exacerbated by the increasing aversion to conflict that has evolved in many organizations. Because feedback is a key ingredient of such appraisals, and feedback often assumes some conflict, the function has been diminished as simplistic scorecards and checklists push meaningful dialogue off the management table. Effective facilitation demands goal setting, listening, feedback, and problem solving, but these skills are seldom taught to supervisors.

9. The ability to assess a situation and create an effective design for a group, team, or individual. ☐

The reason this value-based behavior is number nine out of 10 is the other skills are a prerequisite to be successful at design. The goal of this book is to provide facilitators with a new way of thinking about how they assess any situation and then act on their assessment. This new approach also includes a sample of some of the classic designs to build upon, thus expanding their repertoire.

10. Your ability to deal with wide-ranging conflicts in real time. ☐

Handling conflict effectively demands the ability to assess the needs of a conflict situation and then design an effective solution in real time. It is the test of whether you have internalized the knowledge of this small book. Without training, most of us use the same conflict resolution strategies that we learned from our families, who probably didn't know how to deal with conflict, either. Because a large part of a facilitator's role involves either conflict or change, this skill is what some would call the kicker, demanding the use of the other behaviors in some form or another.

These 10 behavioral abilities have the facilitator doing something to improve the outcome, motivation, or action of others, using a principle—behavioral skill—thought to be essential. While performance management is traditionally a management function, it involves the deepest kind of listening and empathy, and the clearest feedback, goal setting, and visioning possible. It is the ultimate in facilitation. And conflict and how it is resolved will most certainly raise its ugly head along the way.

For the facilitator, intentionality in each one of these behaviors is essential while considering the consequences of your own actions—again, often in real time. And all these facilitating actions demand your willingness to scrutinize your own impact in light of your intentions.

PART II

EXECUTION

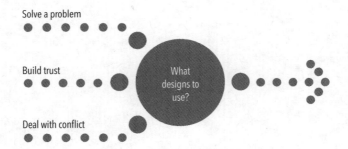

From our catalog of more than 100 designs, we have chosen 13 that have reso-nated most with our clients. They're also the ones we have found most user friendly. These designs address the challenges facilitators face all the time: problem identification and priority setting, building trust among a team, dealing with difficult people, bringing issues to the table for discussion, posing tough ques-tions to an intimidating leader, and providing feedback to team members.

All the designs ensure safety for the participants, but they also have a degree of shared risk that tends to build greater cohesion among the team. They are of suffi-cient variety that together, they will give you the tools and skills to begin crafting your own diagnostically sound designs for your groups and teams.

Long ago, we discovered that only the rare facilitator will risk using a design of any kind without experiencing it first. With this book and our accompanying animated videos, we can now provide facilitators with the experience of a well-crafted design—without having to guide them through it in person. Our use of animated characters lets you see exactly how to apply the design, almost as if you were there. They demonstrate how easy the implementation of virtually any design is, even for a novice facilitator, leader, manager, or consultant. Through the animation, not only can you witness what to do, but you will also hear a description of each step with tips and insights into why things are done in a particular way, which will speed you toward a successful outcome.

5

SOLVING PROBLEMS AND SETTING PRIORITIES

This first group of designs addresses the most common team activities we find in the working environment—solving problems and figuring out what to do first, with our ever-shrinking time and personnel resources. Problem solving on an individual basis is relatively straightforward—you just have to make a decision (or a series of decisions) and then see it through. Simple. But group problem solving is an entirely different animal. Without facilitation, even a group that is highly skilled in problem-solving techniques will struggle to make decisions efficiently, because we are all human beings with our own agendas, egos, and ways of seeing the world. The facilitator's role is crucial in both mediating individual personalities and keeping the group on track.

There are many approaches you can take to complete these activities, but the ones we are about to show you are different in that they engage the brainpower of the whole team. This is built on the assumption that most groups are undisciplined when they engage in a group-oriented problem-solving discussion. Not only do a few people tend to dominate the discussion, but some individuals are often in a hurry and leap prematurely to predetermined decisions, wasting the group's time justifying their ideas. Any good problem-solving process provides a structured approach that first diagnoses the problem and then ensures a rigorous discussion among the participants. This usually demands a facilitator who can guide the team through a step-by-step process and allows a thoughtful process to unfold. And they must help the group decide on an effective decision-making process so that no one person or small cabal of individuals can manipulate the situation. Thus, the facilitator acts as guide, arbiter, and educator of the group, helping to establish rules of engagement that can keep the members on track.

We believe in having choices to fit the needs found in most efforts of group problem solving. Here we provide five methods, all with unique selling points. Take time to familiarize yourself with all the designs, their strengths and their limitations, and the different skills and behaviors to which the participants will be introduced. All these are important factors to bear in mind when the time comes to decide which design you will use. Also, your familiarity with all aspects of these designs will expand your capacity to eventually create your own designs to meet the unique needs of teams or groups you work with.

Future Search

The Future Search design (Figure 5-1) takes its name from seeking out all-new possibilities for a better future by canvassing ideas from a large number of people (ranging from eight to 40) in a short amount of time. It is also known as the Interview Design or Speed Dating because of its layout. It is one of the easiest designs to facilitate as a novice because it is so structured. You do not have to be a charismatic facilitator. The process is highly engaging and grabs the interest of the participants as long as the problem is relevant and the diagnostic questions are stimulating and interesting. Follow the structure and you are guaranteed a positive result and a fun experience. But be warned—miss a step and you may have trouble. Thus, while the design can be used with many kinds of problems, it does have a stepwise process that has to be followed. So, please be extra careful to follow the detailed instructions, because this process can be very challenging to explain to participants.

The design is a creative way to collect and organize ideas from your team, by having them "speed date" their way through a series of up to six questions. It can be used as a diagnostic tool within a team or larger organization to uncover difficult issues, while also beginning the exploration of solutions to those issues. It is adaptable to a wide range of situations, is easy to replicate once the design is understood, and perhaps most important, it's enjoyable for those participating. We know this because our meeting evaluations show this design consistently receiving the highest

Figure 5-1. Future Search

Design 1: The Future Search

marks. Following is a demonstration of how to harness the collective brainpower of your team in five easy steps.

Let's use an example: Imagine that you are a facilitator within a division of a large service organization. Six months ago, there was a reorganization of this larger organization that led to some negative influences in both productivity and morale within your division. Many of your leaders are dissatisfied with the new organization and severe restrictions on spending that came with it; while they understand the financial constraints, they also want to do something to fix the situation. You have been asked to facilitate a session using the Future Search design to help these top leaders remedy some of the issues.

Step 1: The Pre-Work

You schedule a half day for your team of leaders, realizing that this may be the first of several sessions required to resolve the issues. You believe the Future Search design will initiate a process of true engagement, after a period of top-down crisis reactive management during the months following the reorganization. Given the acknowledged problems in the transition period, you ask the leaders of the organization to each submit an anonymous list of the six issues they believe need to be addressed by the group in the half-day session. From that information, you craft six questions that will provide the focus of the group's effort.

Here are some example questions based on this organization:

1. What factors in the current reorganization are not working and need to be addressed? Please be specific.
2. What advice would you give [the division boss] as they attempt to improve the organization's effectiveness?
3. What factors are undermining our productivity?
4. Given the challenges of the past few months, what are three things you would do immediately to increase morale?
5. We've been told that communications have suffered as of late. What would you suggest specifically to remedy this situation?
6. What are the two toughest questions we should be addressing as a division, but people might be reluctant to ask?

The questions must be challenging, relevant, interesting, and able to be answered by the participants in a short amount of time.

Step 2: The Setup

There will be 24 participants for the session, and you arrange the large room with the chairs in four rows of six, facing each other and close together (Figure 5-2). It is important that the chairs stay close together throughout the design. We have found this provides the participants a more personal experience, almost as if they are sharing a secret. On each chair, you have placed a pad of paper, a pen, and a sheet of paper with a single question lying facedown. The format for the question sheets is

Figure 5-2. Future Search Setup

the question number, the actual question, and a large letter X or O. The X or O simply denotes which row the question sheet will be placed on and will be helpful later, when we describe to the participants who should be doing what. As you will see in the detail of the design, there will always be an equal number of Xs and Os.

Step 3: The Speed Dating

Ask the participants (who have having been waiting in another room, with coffee and snacks), to sit in any chair, but not to look at their questions yet.

Explain that they each have a question numbered from 1 to 6. Also, on their question sheet they have a large letter X or O. Those who have an X on their paper will, when you say go, lean forward to the person sitting across from them and read their question to the individual (an O person) and, at the same time, show it to them. Some people have an easier time processing the question when they can read it, while others do better when it is read to them, so it's important to include both options (Figure 5-3).

TOP TIP If one of the six questions is about the boss, do not place participants in the position of having to answer that particular question directly to the boss. Make sure the boss has a different question to ask.

The individual receiving the question will then have three minutes to answer the question as best they can. In the first three-minute round, all the Xs will be listening at once. Then in the second round, all the Os will be listening and the Xs sharing their responses to the question—so be prepared for the room to get noisy.

As the facilitator, encourage the interviewers (those asking the questions) to probe for examples, getting the best information possible. All the information gathered is anonymous, therefore no names will be attached to any statements made. It is important to emphasize this, especially when the group has lost some trust, as in this example. Also, tell the group that later each participant will search for patterns among the data they have written down; thus, taking good notes is important.

At the end of the first three-minute round, indicate that it's time to switch, and the people in the O row will then ask their question to the X person. Again, it is best that they both read and show the question and seek examples whenever possible.

Figure 5-3. Each Participant Will Ask One of Six Questions

After the second three-minute round, have the participants rotate. The people in the *O* row will move one chair to their left. The person at the end will move around to the back end of their row, as you can see in Figure 5-4. The people in the *X* row will remain still throughout the process, and everyone keeps their same question for the next round.

Once all the *O*s have moved, start the next round of three minutes, with the *X*s asking their question to a new individual. This process continues until the *X*s have had the opportunity to talk to every person in the opposite row.

Figure 5-4. O Row Movement

TOP TIP Make sure that the chairs stay close together once people have moved. Some people will try to shuffle themselves farther apart while you are not looking, because they are uncomfortable being in such close proximity to others.

Tell the participants that at some point they will have the opportunity to answer their own question because every question is duplicated. This means they should focus on capturing only what other people say—without putting their own spin on things.

It is important to give the directions twice. While nothing in the directions is particularly difficult to understand, it might be an unusual event for the participants. Also expect to answer many questions about the process and who should be doing what and when.

Step 4: Organizing the Data

In about an hour (including the setup, explanations, and all the moving around), the Future Search process provides a complete sample from those present. Now the challenge is to make sense of the information. Ask the participants to take another 20 minutes to individually organize the data from their question. A best practice is to use the process of truths, trends, and unique ideas—the same process that you'll see in other designs such as Genie in the Bottle or The Carousel.

Truths: A truth is a response to a question that cannot be denied. It is mentioned or agreed to by at least four of the six individuals interviewed. It is so powerful that it seems to leap off the page. Sometimes there is no truth. In the situation in our example, one would anticipate that some truths will exist.

Trends: A trend is mentioned by two or three of those interviewed and if not addressed might turn into a truth or become a bigger problem in the future.

Unique Ideas: A unique idea is one that the interviewer believes is important to discuss, adds dimension to a problem, or warrants further examination. Clearly this can be a somewhat subjective process. Nevertheless, such creative and potentially valuable ideas shouldn't be lost. Often brilliance does not come from the view of the majority.

Step 5: The Presentation

Once the participants have organized their data individually, you should create new groups of four, based on the question numbers people have been working with. All the individuals who interviewed with question 1 will get together, share their conclusions, and reach a consensus about the information to be presented to the larger group. If one person has an issue as a trend and another has it as a truth, the group of four must negotiate for the final categorization. If they can't come to some agreement, the idea won't be presented. The negotiations take about 20 minutes, and at the end, each group of four will have agreed on one set of truths, trends, and unique ideas that they believe must be presented to the larger group and reflects the current reality for that organization.

Then each presenting group selects the most important issue that they agree must be addressed to present to the large group. Again, they need to agree on which one. To make this issue memorable, they design a brief three- to five-minute skit or vignette that demonstrates it. It can be a serious or humorous depiction of the issue, and they can use props, exaggerate—whatever will make it resonate with the group. This should take about 20 minutes to design. Asking people to design a skit may generate a bit of resistance, because it forces people to choose a difficult issue and puts them into a performance role. The surprise is that these vignettes tend to be the most memorable parts of the entire activity.

Finally, each group has about five minutes to present their information to the large group. They read their question. Then, without discussion, they present their skit. And then, one or more people present the truths, trends, and unique ideas for their question.

It is not uncommon for similar issues to arise from very different questions. Obviously uncovering the issues is the first step. You will need to schedule additional follow-up work to figure out what to do to address these issues, but you could immediately take a quick vote to try to prioritize them. Planning a follow-up activity using a design like our 6-Step Problem Solving would be a good way to engage the group in solving them, whether immediately or at a later date. While this is primarily a diagnostic design, some of the responses may have solutions embedded in them.

Here is a summary of the steps with the time needed for each.

Step 1: The Pre-Work	60 Minutes (before the session)
Step 2: The Setup	30 Minutes (before the session)
Step 3: The Speed Dating	60 Minutes
Step 4: Organizing the Data	20 Minutes

Step 5: The Presentation   70 Minutes
Total Design: **2.5 Hours**

The Carousel

The Carousel (Figure 5-5) is a simple yet creative design for engaging up to 30 people in problem solving by seeking their answers to as many as six challenging questions. One of the concerns with group problem solving is that participants can show up with the solution already in their minds. When this happens, it can be difficult for people to hear solutions different from their own cunning plans. The trick for facilitators is to expect this to happen, and to have a great design up their sleeves to deal with it. There are two things in particular you need to watch out for:

1. If you put people in a group and tell them to explore solutions to a problem without first uncovering all the underlying causes, you may generate solutions that might be fixing the wrong problem.
2. It is important that you harness the collective brainpower in the room by making sure you hear all the different perspectives of those present.

If we can do this without a few people dominating the discussion, then we are giving ourselves the best chance of creating truly brilliant solutions. The Carousel design is just the ticket for achieving this.

Figure 5-5. The Carousel

Design 2: The Carousel

Step 1: The Pre-Work

As in the Future Search design, the first step is about creating powerful questions that will be used to challenge the group. Do not underestimate how important this step is. The quality of your questions will dictate how successful the problem solving actually is.

 TOP TIP Carefully choose a couple of people to help you craft the questions. You need to use people you can trust and who know the situation well enough to be honest about what the real issues are.

Let's use an example to demonstrate how to create really great questions. Two small companies have recently merged. The financial and business rationale for the merger is sound. But, as often is the case, the merging of the two cultures has proven to be a challenge. The new leader decides to use the Carousel design to get people talking about the kind of culture they should be striving for in the new business. He engages a couple of highly trusted leaders from each of the two former companies, and together they create six tough questions to be addressed by the group:

1. **What behaviors do you believe must be part of our new company to ensure a climate of trust and candor?** This question sets out to reveal culture, trust, and candor, which are not things you can easily see. If the question asks about behavior, then the answers to the question will demonstrate the invisible culture you are looking for.

2. **Given our fresh start, what dysfunctional behaviors have you experienced previously that you hope are not part of our new company?** This question works because you are not asking them to "out" anybody doing anything dysfunctional—it's a question focused on the future that they can all answer.

3. **What sources of stress should we try to diminish as we move forward?** People love to talk about their stress, but rarely do they get a chance to do something about it.

4. **In any merger, there are barriers that can reduce success. Which of these do you think are affecting us and how?** This question helps set the tone because it assumes that such barriers will occur and people are experiencing them now. Thus, people are safe to talk about them because they are systemic.

5. **What have you most valued about people from the other organization?** This question forces people to look for positives from the other side, which helps get people out of their entrenched positions.

6. **If you were the leader, what would you and your new leadership team need to do differently to be truly high performing?** This is a good question because people love to criticize and give advice to their leaders.

The final part of step 1 is to decide who will be attending the meeting. It is essential to choose enough people from different parts of the organization to provide an end-to-end view of the problem you are trying to solve. In the example, the new leader invites a selection of 18 individuals from each former organization, the bulk of the new leadership team, and perhaps a few suppliers or customers who have longstanding relationships with each of the old companies.

Step 2: The Setup

Arrange for a large open room without tables. Place six easels at various points around the room, perhaps 20 feet apart. Place chairs around each easel, according to the size of the group you have. If your group is 18 people, divide that by six questions and you will have three chairs per easel. On each easel, write the station number (1, 2, 3, 4, 5, or 6) on the top flipchart page, then turn the page over, and write the corresponding question on the next sheet. Don't forget to turn back over to the number page once you are done writing the question, and make sure you leave plenty of masking tape and markers at each easel (Figure 5-6). Repeat until you have set up all your questions.

Place enough additional chairs to seat everybody, either at one end of the room or in a separate room, depending on your venue size. When the participants arrive, ask them to sit in these chairs for a 10- to 15-minute introduction. It is important that the leader provides this introduction, even if you or someone else is facilitating the design. This shows the group that the leader is committed to both the process and the outcome. They need to set the scene for the problem to be solved, give as much context as possible, and encourage the group to be completely honest.

Step 3: The Carousel

Now it's time for the facilitator to set the design in motion. Tell the group that in order to explore what their new culture needs to be, you've developed six questions.

Figure 5-6. Carousel Setup

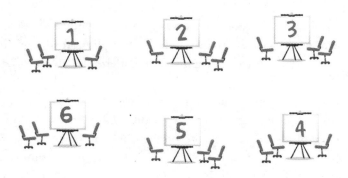

Tell them that in a moment they will move over to the working area, where they will find six numbered easels, each containing one question. After this brief explanation, divide the group into six groups of three—the more random the better, but also with a good mix of people from the two previous organizations. Have three to five individuals at each easel.

Ask everyone to go to their assigned easel. Expect at this point for people to be moving in all directions, and a few to not move at all, looking confused. Your job as the facilitator is to keep calm, repeat the directions clearly, and generally help shepherd them all to the six new subgroups. Once they are all in position, tell them they will have 10 minutes to take turns writing down all their answers for this question, before they move on to the next question. If one person, for example, has three ideas, the second person can make a check mark next to any idea that is similar to their own (instead of writing the idea down again), and then write down

TOP TIP Try to identify the most outspoken or influential people—and in this example, which of the two organizations people are from—before you implement the design. This is so you can discreetly tweak the makeup of the subgroups to ensure a balance of assertive people in each one. A good way of doing this would be to prepare name tags for everyone and print their subgroup numbers on the back. If they ask how the groups were selected, simply tell them that you attempted to ensure heterogeneity.

their "new" or additional ideas. The third member would then follow suit, checking off any ideas they have in common, and adding any additional ideas.

You can also suggest that they nominate one person to scribe in their subgroup and capture one idea at a time from each person, so they all get a chance to contribute from the get-go (Figure 5-7). Once they are clear on the instructions, tell them to turn over the page and start answering their question.

Figure 5-7. Answering the First Question

After this first 10 minutes, regardless of whether they've finished, tell the subgroups to move to the next easel to their right (Figure 5-8). Tell them they now have 10 minutes to add their new ideas to the information already captured by the previous subgroup. If they agree with any statements already on the sheet, they should again make a check mark against these. Having each group write in a different color can be a good idea so you can see the differences in input as they are created. It's a good idea for each group to have a different individual start the process for each round.

Keep the subgroups moving around until they end up at the easel where they started. They will probably need to use several sheets of paper, so tell them to stick any filled sheets on the wall and start a new sheet. As the design progresses, you can normally shorten the time spent at each easel, because there is less to write down. If all the groups have finished writing at, say, seven minutes, you can tell them to move on—so make sure you are paying attention as they finish.

Please note that the way this section is explained is intentional: The instructions were very clear and concise, they were given in very small chunks, and only at the exact time they were needed by the participants. People who are not used to working in this way might either misunderstand what is required of them, or just flat-out panic. Running the design in this way will greatly reduce the amount of chaos—and help you make sure the participants have fun in the process. In many new groups, it's difficult for some people to ask clarifying questions because they don't want to feel stupid.

Figure 5-8. Groups Moving Around the Room

Step 4: The Summarization

Each of the six subgroups now has 20 minutes to create a one-page summary of the information provided on the sheets for their question (this is the one they started with and are now once again standing in front of). They must identify the areas of greatest agreement and any unique statements that are important to them. For example, a brilliant idea may have been posted toward the end, and there might be only a few check marks of agreement. If the members of the original group believe the idea is worthy of being presented to the larger group, then they can make certain this happens by adding more check marks to it. The idea is to have a list in some order of importance that is composed of discrete issues that need to be addressed.

Similarly, the original subgroup may have new ideas of their own to add after completing the whole circuit. As they go through the summarization process, the main guideline is that all members of the subgroup must agree on what is presented to the larger group. It might make sense to organize the data into truths, trends, and unique ideas, using the process described in the Future Search design. This is the facilitator's call.

Step 5: The Report Back

The subgroups have five minutes to present their one page of conclusions to the entire group and take questions as necessary. This is not the time to debate the findings, but an opportunity to clarify the points being presented.

Step 6: The "So What"

The leaders are now armed with a range of suggestions and beliefs in relation to the questions posed. You, as facilitator, will need to have the division leader close the meeting, making sure they thank the participants for their time, ideas, and honesty. They also need to explain that this is a great starting point and to specify what will happen next with their data. It is common for facilitators to forget this final point.

You could plan to immediately engage this same group in turning their data into specific recommendations and action plans by choosing a follow-up activity from one of the other 12 designs. Or, you could do this later, perhaps with a different group. Either way, detailed strategies will need to be developed to bring these initial ideas to fruition. You (with the leader's blessing) could also develop a task force—one person chosen by members from each group. These six and the boss would meet with the facilitator's help to frame the issues generated in each of the six groups. How and when these issues would be addressed can differ, but often this group becomes a design group for further problem solving. This is a good way to educate others in the organization with concepts of design. If you take this approach, ensure that these ideas are reported back to all the participants of the original Carousel activity.

The biggest error that the leader of this event could make is to not act after such a collaborative process. As the facilitator, you might want to remind them of this fact and the disillusionment and cost to group morale this would create.

Here is a summary of the steps with the time needed for each.

Step 1: The Pre-Work	Up to 60 Minutes (before the session)
Step 2: The Setup	15 Minutes (not including setup)
Step 3: The Carousel	45 Minutes
Step 4: The Summarization	20 Minutes
Step 5: The Report Back	30 Minutes
Step 6: The "So What"	10 Minutes
Total Design:	**2 Hours**

Collapsing Consensus

The Collapsing Consensus (Figure 5-9) is a simple but incredibly effective design for collecting and organizing ideas from a group that cleverly ensures a high degree of engagement from participants. The design can be used in many different ways, such as a stand-alone event or as part of a more complex design strategy. Its use can make any facilitator stronger, because it can move a stalled group toward action, be a useful diagnostic, help in creating consensus, ensure greater participation from low talkers (while limiting the participation of those who predictably hog center stage), and optimize the use of everyone's limited time. It can be used with as few as four people and with as many as 100—and so it is a critical part of your design repertoire.

Figure 5-9. Collapsing Consensus

Design 3:
Collapsing
Consensus

Basically, it's a listing process. So many times, a starting point of problem solving includes having a group make a list of possibilities or, perhaps, a list of issues. You can start by brainstorming, but our experience shows that in a group of, say, eight to 10 people, two or three will dominate the session. This is because these two or three might react faster than others, or are less reserved, and others will keep quiet out of habit, respect, intimidation, or annoyance: "Why bother? There they go again; just let them do it."

We have discovered over many years and considerable trial and error that clusters of three or four are optimal for ensuring maximum participation in a listing process. However, even when we use clusters of four, good ideas might still be lost because some individuals don't respond well under pressure, or one super enthusiastic individual gives their ideas while the other three pull back. Using a tool called the Nominal Technique (step 2) within our Collapsing Consensus design can improve the responses dramatically.

Step 1: The Setup

Split your group into clusters of four—the magic number. If your group does not evenly divide into four, you can use a bit of artistic license and have a left-over trio or a pair to make it work.

 Find out who the most outspoken or influential people are before you execute the design so you can discreetly tweak the makeup of the clusters to limit their power. For example, you could put two high talkers in the same group so they cancel each other out, allowing more participation in the other groups.

Let's consider an example group of salespeople from a small medical supply company. There are 13 people in the group, and you divide them into four clusters—A, B, C, and D (Figure 5-10). You could have three groups of three people and one of four, but you need to put your two high talkers together to minimize their domination effects on the whole group. So in this case, we have two groups of four, a trio, and a pair.

Figure 5-10. The Example Group

Step 2: The Nominal Technique

Here's an example question to help demonstrate the nominal technique: "List all the reasons sales have declined by 30 percent since this time last year." Tell the group to do this first individually in their notebooks, with no talking, and give everyone five minutes to write their top 10 ideas.

Then, nominate one person in each cluster to act as a scribe who will go around their cluster taking one idea at a time from everyone. The scribe will post each idea on a flipchart until all the ideas are captured. If others in the cluster have the same idea, this can be shown by putting one or more check marks next to the idea (Figure 5-11). Give them 10 minutes to capture their ideas.

With our group of 13, we could conceivably get 130 responses. But by putting people in their clusters to work, the numbers are often reduced to about 10 or 12 ideas per cluster, because there will be considerable overlap.

SCALING THE DESIGN

The nominal technique can also be used with a single large group of 10 to 15 people, by asking only for each individual's top five ideas. Limiting the number of ideas per person like this can still potentially give us 50-plus ideas, but it is manageable due to the many duplicates that will occur and the agreement you will get on themes.

Figure 5-11. Capturing Ideas From the Cluster

Step 3: The Prioritization of Ideas in Each Cluster

Now that each of your clusters has a list of ideas, it's time to prioritize them. Give each cluster 15 minutes to agree on the best four ideas on their list. In the process, they must create a rationale for why these are the best. It's OK if cluster members negotiate to enlist support for one idea or another. For example, a member could say something like, "I'm willing to go with idea number three if you can buy idea number nine." If the cluster can't agree on four, have them present the ones they can agree to, but no more than four in the time available.

Step 4: The Collapsing Consensus

Now it's time for the design to get to work. Ask clusters A and B to come together, and clusters C and D to similarly join. Give each new group 20 minutes to do the following: Cluster A will show their four prioritized ideas to B and present why each is important. B members can ask questions for clarification but not for debate. Then, B will give A their four ideas in a similar fashion (Figure 5-12).

There's almost always at least one item of agreement. If not, cluster A will look for areas of "gentle agreement" on the other team's list—ideas that resonate with them. The goal is to negotiate as a group until they can agree on a single list of four.

Meanwhile, the same process occurs among members of C and D clusters, with them eventually agreeing on their four best ideas. All group members must agree on any idea that makes their final list, meaning they are willing to live with all the ideas that make it.

Figure 5-12. The Collapsing Consensus

Step 5: The Las Vegas Vote, With a Twist

After groups A and B have agreed on their top four ideas, and groups C and D also have their list of four, have them all come together once again. Individuals from the AB group will now be asked to advocate (with some passion) for one idea from the CD group's list. Repeat with individuals from the CD group advocating for one idea from the AB group's list. This can be very challenging for individuals who are particularly entrenched in their own solutions or believe that the other cluster is wrong. The purpose of this is to remind people that the group is after the best for the whole and it's not a win-lose situation. This is the twist. Make sure the advocating from each individual goes pretty quickly—ideally about 30 seconds per person.

Then, give each individual 10 points that they can distribute across the eight ideas as they wish (Figure 5-13). If they want, they can put all 10 points on one idea—it's up to them. This is the Las Vegas Vote; it is slightly different from a regular vote because the participants can place all their votes on one idea to sway opinion in a particular direction. It is akin to going all in on a particular number of the roulette wheel. The result of the vote will give the large group some sense of which items have the greatest support, to help prioritize areas of further work. As a final, alternative twist to the vote, you could ask each individual to place at least three votes on ideas that did *not* come from their cluster or subgroup. It depends how much you want to challenge the participants to rally behind ideas other than their own.

Figure 5-13. The Las Vegas Vote

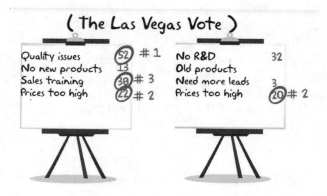

Here is a summary of the steps with the time needed for each.

Step 1: The Setup	5 Minutes
Step 2: The Nominal Technique	15 Minutes
Step 3: The Prioritization of Ideas in Each Cluster	15 Minutes
Step 4: The Collapsing Consensus	20 Minutes
Step 5: The Las Vegas Vote, With a Twist	20 Minutes
Total Design:	**75 Minutes**

SCALING THE DESIGN

In this example, we used a group of 13 people. It would be pretty much the same design with as many as 40 members, resulting in 10 groups of four. With a larger group like this, you would keep collapsing the clusters together, multiple times, until you end up with no more than about 12 ideas for the whole group to consider. Also, to save time, we encourage only a couple of people to advocate for each of the final 12 or so ideas. The vote then occurs as before, with each individual spreading their 10 points across the final ideas.

Executives and the Common Person

The Executives and the Common Person design is based on one undeniable fact: The more people feel engaged in their organizations, the better their performance will be in terms of productivity, morale, and profit. Here, engagement represents increasing the collaboration of people with higher-level managers, participating in solving problems that influence their work lives, and having their opinions sought in their areas of expertise (Figure 5-14). Engagement is synonymous with involvement and purposeful behavior. The question is, how can leaders increase feelings of engagement so they can reap the benefits of higher productivity and performance?

Figure 5-14. Executives and the Common Person

Design 4: Executives and the Common Person

Executive Team
10 People

Directors
35 People

Managers
150 People

Production Associates
1,000 People

This design, although complex and time consuming, has proven to increase engagement, due to the executive team reaching out to other leaders down the chain of command. It works because people love to talk, love to be experts, and love to respond to important questions. However, the questions being asked must help gain information leaders truly want, and the data must be used in meaningful ways.

Step 1: The Setup

Good questions are the key to meaningful answers, and the way to create good questions is to invest in designing them. Let's use an example company: Gravitron is a high-tech manufacturing company with good performance, but the executive team now want to take this to the next level and truly engage their associates to help achieve superior results. The company has a well-regarded executive team of 10, 35 directors at the next level down, then 150 managers, and finally 1,000 production associates (Figure 5-15). Because you are an experienced facilitator within the company, your help has been requested to design a way for the executives to learn what is really going on, and what needs to be done to make the company better.

Figure 5-15. Gravitron Management Hierarchy

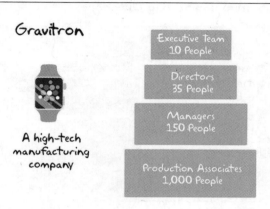

First, ask everyone in the top two tiers of the organization for their five toughest questions that need to be answered about the current state of the organization. A good way of ensuring participation is to have the executive team explain the project and how much they value everyone's input. If the request for help comes directly and personally from each individual's manager, the likelihood that people will respond increases greatly. Once you get the 45 or so responses from this group, select a representative sample of the people involved to help sort the questions. In Gravitron's case, the facilitator might make up three groups of two executives and four or five directors to review the questions and decide on the top five to be used for the organizational assessment sought by the leadership team (Figure 5-16).

Here are some sample questions the groups might select:
- What are things we should be doing but aren't that would strengthen us as an effective manufacturing organization?
- What are things we should stop doing to increase our effectiveness?
- If you were the boss, what two things would you do immediately to improve morale? The more specific, the better.

- On a 10-point scale, with 1 being low, how much do you believe your opinions are solicited in your area of work interest? Please explain.
- Respect is one of our five core values. On a 10-point scale, to what degree do you feel respected in your role as a member of this work community? Please explain.

Figure 5-16. Gathering and Sorting Questions

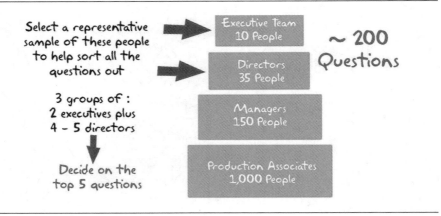

 TOP TIP When you choose the top five questions, make sure you have some scaled questions as well as open-ended ones. This will help greatly when it comes to making sense of all the data.

Step 2: The Interviews

Divide up the organization from director level downward into groups of about 10 people from all different levels. In this case, you would have more than 100 groups, each with possibly a director, one or two managers, and eight or nine production associates. Then divide these groups so that you give each executive team member 11 or 12 groups to interview, with the list of five questions we identified in step 1. Each executive will then ask all five questions to each of their interview groups, holding 11 or 12 focus group–style meetings to get the data collected (Figure 5-17).

Because you are acting as a consultant when facilitating this process, it's a good idea for you to interview the members of the executive team with the same five questions. You can then compare their responses with the other data you'll receive.

Figure 5-17. The Interviews

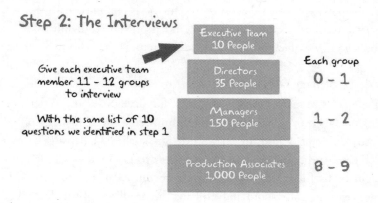

Step 2: The Interviews

Give each executive team member 11 – 12 groups to interview

With the same list of 10 questions we identified in step 1

Executive Team
10 People

Directors
35 People

Managers
150 People

Production Associates
1,000 People

Each group

0 – 1

1 – 2

8 – 9

TOP TIP When you assign the groups to each executive team member, make sure they are not interviewing people directly in their chain of command.

Step 3: Compiling the Data

With more than 100 interviews, each consisting of five questions, you are going to end up with a ton of data. If you can, engage the executive team to help make sense of the information. This will also help when it comes to deciphering their hastily scribbled interview responses and other shorthand.

As the facilitator of this design, you are responsible for determining the best way of tabulating and presenting the data. One way would be to create a spreadsheet for all the scaled items and graph the responses for each question as a bar chart. This will make it clear where the majority of the responses lie and whether there is a big spread in people's experiences. The open-ended data are more difficult to organize. One possibility is to load the responses into a Word document and then use word-cloud software, available online, to create a word cloud for each question. Another option would be to turn the open-ended data into scaled data by assigning the responses to themes and then counting the number of hits for each theme. Finally, you might have associates within your company who are good at organizing data, so if this is not your forte, find somebody to help you.

Once you have figured out how best to present the data and have developed templates for capturing them, put the executive team members into pairs and teach them how to organize their data. If you are going to use the executives to help you organize the data, you must make sure the methods you choose are easy to understand, easy to use, and produce similar data independent of individual skill level. This comes back to how you design the data capture templates up front—so be aware.

Step 4: Making Meaning

Bring the executive team together and look for similarities and differences across the different data sets. What are the common themes? Where are people's experiences vastly different? Choosing another design, such as Collapsing Consensus, or a method like truths, trends, and unique ideas to help with making sense of the data might be useful at this point. Make sure you create a summary of the findings that is easy to understand and explains the headlines of the data to be shared across the entire organization. This will provide transparency around the process and reassure people that their opinions have been heard.

Step 5: The "So What"

This step is all about establishing the organizational priorities: what to do first to make things better. Get the executive team together to determine which themes are the most important to them, and under each theme, which actions will make the biggest impact (Figure 5-18). At this stage, keep the actions to a very high level; later, each will likely require their own designs to problem solve and fully define the details.

Figure 5-18. The "So What"

80

It will be hard to decide on only two or three things to work on in the short term, but you must get them to be disciplined in choosing these. If you try to do it all at once, then the organization will be overwhelmed. The Las Vegas Vote, With a Twist would help with this decision making.

Step 6: Closing the Loop

Once the priorities and action plans have been established, schedule a series of town hall–type meetings to communicate them throughout the organization. To make this process less arduous, you can use the pairs of executive team members from step 3 to lead the different meetings. Make sure you think about how to make these meetings more engaging than a traditional town hall. For example, using the News Conference design (which we'll cover later in the book) would be a great way to engage the participants in asking questions in a safe environment. Most town hall meetings are not done well at all. They are not easy meetings to facilitate to engage the sheer number of people who attend, so invest the time necessary to design the communication meeting well. Not many executives can present their data in a manner that feels authentic and is effective in communicating the true feelings of the organization. As the facilitator, you will need to help the executive team get this piece right; otherwise, the meeting could feel manipulative or like the executives didn't really want to hear the feedback they received.

Whatever design you choose for the town hall, try to communicate the priorities and action plans a few days prior to the meeting, so that people have time to digest them and prepare any questions. The town hall meeting then becomes much more interactive than a traditional information broadcast, and the questions asked much more meaningful. After all this effort invested in this design, wouldn't you rather have an exciting presentation of the process and results, with lots of exciting questions?

Here is a summary of the steps with the time needed for each.

Step 1: The Setup	7 Days
Step 2: The Interviews	7 Days
Step 3: Compiling the Data	4 Days
Step 4: Making Meaning	1 Day
Step 5: The "So What"	1 Day
Step 6: Closing the Loop	4 Days
Total Design:	**24 Days**

6-Step Problem Solving

6-Step Problem Solving is an adaptable and creative means of solving a problem, while dramatically reducing the possibility of conflict in a group. There are hundreds of approaches to problem solving, and many can be used successfully in group settings. This design not only solves the problem, but does so while building a greater sense of trust through collaboration (Figure 5-19). And you can use the design individually, or in groups of two, 10, or even 20. It is that adaptable.

You can complete this design in an hour, or it could take several. It depends on what you are trying to solve. Two hours is usually enough for most problems, but make sure this is enough time to fully cover all the issues. Please note that if the group is completely unskilled in problem solving or the problem is especially contentious, this activity might take closer to three hours to complete.

Figure 5-19. 6-Step Problem Solving

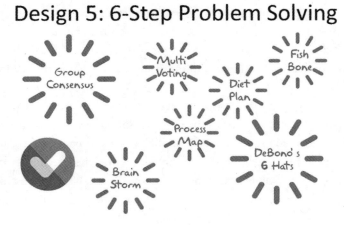

Ensure that you have enough physical space to be able to work in smaller groups, with each subgroup having some wall space, a flipchart on an easel, markers, and tape (Figure 5-20) for displaying the ongoing work of the problem-solving process.

Let's use an example for demonstrating the 6-Step Problem Solving design. A small college has been losing increasing numbers of students after their second year. The impact on the college is approaching $1.5 million annually in lost revenues. There has also been an impact on morale of the remaining students and faculty, leading to reduced levels of productivity on both sides. A group of four faculty members, three administrators, three students, and two recent alumni have been selected to assess the problem and make specific recommendations for improvement.

The facilitator's first job is to establish a clear problem statement from which to work. This defines the condition that exists and needs to be addressed. It is stated objectively, descriptively, and as specifically as possible. The more specific the problem, the easier it is to attack. Develop an initial statement for the group, like this one: "An increasing number of students are leaving the college between their first and second years."

Figure 5-20. Supplies for Working Group

TOP TIP Make sure the statement does not identify whether the reality of the condition is good or bad or suggest what things would be like if the problem were solved. Beginning with a description of the current reality reduces the tendency to jump prematurely to solutions, prior to the hard work of the diagnosis. The statement is the first step in the problem-solving process.

Divide the group into clusters of three and ask them to discuss the problem statement for about five minutes. This can lead to changes in the statement, or some clarification. Both are good. Next, the facilitator should give a preview of the six steps:

- Step 1: The Diagnostic
- Step 2: The Benefits
- Step 3: The Blocks
- Step 4: Dealing With Emotion
- Step 5: Generating Alternatives
- Step 6: Next Steps

It's important to set some ground rules up front before you dive into the steps. Things like sticking to each step, in order, and not criticizing one another's input or ideas will reduce almost all of the argument and acrimony that can occur. There are many more that the group can generate.

Now divide the group into three different subgroups with a balanced mix of the participants: faculty, administrators, students, and alumni (Figure 5-21). These might be different groups from before because you now want to ensure that they are homogeneous in their makeup. (The representation of the initial groups does not matter because the purpose is just to increase the amount of talking among the participants.)

Figure 5-21. The Subgroups

Step 1: The Diagnostic

Instruct the participants to use the flipchart and list as much as they know about the condition of student attrition. Exactly what is the current reality? Why do they leave? What has changed? Why do people stay? What do people say privately that they might not say publicly? And what other kinds of information might the group need to gather before it can reach a final recommendation?

The groups should remain focused on generating information about the problem and stay away from any premature problem solving or criticism. Encourage them to ask as many questions as they need to within the 20 minutes you've given them. It is helpful to stroll around and be certain that the groups are generating information and not spending time or energy with involved discussions.

At the end of the 20 minutes, ask the groups to select the three most interesting and useful pieces of information they came up with and share these with the whole group. Creating a vivid understanding of the current reality is key to an effective and comprehensive diagnosis.

Step 2: The Benefits

Have the group divide into their subgroups again and take 15 minutes to explore the ideal situation and the benefits to students and the institution if changes were made to the current situation. What exactly would the ideal situation be? What changes must be made from the diagnostic step to move to the ideal state? What would the campus be like if the ideal situation was realized and many of these students stayed? If they were happier? Describe the positive drivers that would propel any change effort forward. It is this discrepancy between the current and ideal realities that creates the tension and motivation to solve the problem.

At the end of the 15 minutes, ask the groups to select the three most interesting and useful pieces of information they came up with and share these with the whole group.

Step 3: The Blocks

Now draw a force field analysis diagram (based on Kurt Lewin's work) on a flipchart, like in Figure 5-22.

Pick an individual problem that would be familiar to people as an example to demonstrate the force field analysis (Figure 5-23). Outline some of the benefits for change on the upward arrows, then suggest a few blocks for the downward arrows. Explain that if the group can create new impetus on the benefits (or upward) side of the equation, then there will be movement. Even better, if they can remove some of the resistances (the downward forces), the balance will change and they will be able to make more progress toward a useful solution.

Figure 5-22. Force Field Analysis

Pick an individual problem as an example to demonstrate to the group:

Losing weight

Not exercising regularly

Ask the subgroups to spend 10 minutes listing the factors blocking the change (getting more students to stay after their first year) on a new piece of flipchart paper.

Once that's done, it's time to get the group thinking in another direction. Ask them to consider this powerful question: What are the benefits of *not* changing? This helps the participants to realize change is not that easy. For example, if an individual is not a smoker anymore, it may change their identity and their accessible social groups. Add this to the force field analysis diagram from before. Now tell them to spend another 10 minutes listing as many benefits to not changing as they can. Tell the groups that this is a difficult but essential question. It is the blocks and the benefits of not changing that keep the ideal state from being reached.

If they appear to be struggling, you can ask if somebody has an example to stimulate everyone's thinking. But be sure to have an example of your own ready, in case everyone is struggling, and you end up being left with no examples.

TOP TIP As they are working on each question, walk among the groups and encourage them to build their lists of responses. Make sure they don't get bogged down in premature solutions or unfocused discussion. The idea is to dig out the factors that cause the identified problem.

Figure 5-23. Force Field Analysis in Action

At the end of the second 10 minutes, ask the groups to select the three most powerful benefits for not changing and share these with the whole group.

Step 4: Dealing With Emotion

At this point, it is more than likely that some strong feelings have risen within people, but they've not yet shared them in their groups. Emotions drive change and the resistance to change. Our experience with change management suggests that people are naturally averse to conflict and emotion, which is why the facilitator should address the pivotal place of emotions in the change process.

Ask the groups to shift gears a bit and move away from the structured, rational way they have been assessing the problem and into another important dimension of problem solving. Have them discuss their strongest feelings about

 **TOP TIP** Check on the groups and stop them from attempting to "solve" each other's feelings. Also, depending on the level of emotion in the room, you might need to let them have a quick break after they have finished this part. It is possible that you will get emotions coming out that have been bottled up for years, so this process can get intense. A break afterward will interrupt the intensity and allow everyone to move on to the next step.

the problem and anything that has occurred to this point. They may have strong positive or negative feelings or emotions about what's happening, or they may not even believe the problem warrants the energy they're putting into it, or any of a hundred other factors that can get their emotions going.

Give them five minutes total in their subgroups to take turns describing how they feel. Anything at all (that is not an attack on another person) is legitimate. It is not a time for discussion, but it is OK for other members of the group to ask clarifying questions. You will find that five minutes can be a long time for people who are not used to talking about their emotions.

Step 5: Generating Alternatives

Tell the groups to stick all their sheets on the wall side by side, so they can see all their data at once. Now have them take about 10 minutes to circle on their sheets the forces that can and must be altered if they are going to change the current condition (Figure 5-24). They should select their top five or six. It's imperative that there is no interest in solving all the underlying issues. At this point, building priorities should be their focus.

Figure 5-24. Generating Alternatives

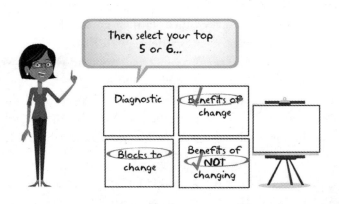

Now take about 30 minutes to write down the most creative next steps the group could take to start solving their top five or six priorities only. Getting them to focus on these will make solving the whole problem much more manageable and stop them from getting overwhelmed. Get them to use all the information they have on their sheets to help generate strategies that will overcome resistance or blocks and move toward the ideal state. Then write the following on flipchart paper:

- What is your goal, or the desired outcome?
- Who is to be involved and responsible for the outcome?
- When is the outcome expected?

Ask the groups to identify all three of these things for each action. Also get them to consider the consequences of any potential solution. What new resistance might result? What other actions would they need to take to overcome this new resistance?

Have each group present their ideas to the other two groups. They can ask any questions for clarification, but not for debate or criticism. Only once every group has presented their ideas can you move to negotiating the very best solutions. Can ideas from different groups be combined to form even more powerful solutions? Does an idea from one group precede another good idea from a different group? The more you can use the ideas to build on one another, the more engaged all the members will be and the more likely the ideas will be implemented. It is impossible to be prescriptive here about how to achieve this, so the facilitator will need to be creative in the moment to get the best results.

Step 6: Next Steps

The problem with problem solving usually occurs during the implementation of our good ideas. Once we leave the meeting, we can easily be swallowed up by other demands and commitments. As the facilitator, you can minimize the risk of this happening by making some plans to consolidate the gains of the problem-solving session and establishing the necessary follow-up.

One way to do this would be to ask each subgroup for a volunteer, then have these people get together to integrate the lists of ideas. They need to be converted to tangible, prioritized actions, with the details of who will be responsible for what and when. These actions would then be presented to senior management in the form of recommendations that simply need to be approved. The more concrete you can make the next steps toward implementation, the greater the chance that senior management will buy in and the ultimate objectives will be met.

Here is a summary of the steps with the time needed for each.

Problem Statement	10 Minutes
Step 1: The Diagnostic	20 Minutes

Step 2: The Benefits	15 Minutes
Step 3: The Blocks	20 Minutes
Step 4: Dealing With Emotion	15 Minutes
Step 5: Generating Alternatives	40 Minutes
Step 6: Next Steps	10 Minutes
Total Design:	**2 Hours and 10 Minutes**

This chapter described five designs that can be used to solve problems and set priorities. While different in approach, they all have common threads. For example, most of these designs will help with data analysis and communication. The very act of experiencing them will improve the team's communication skills and willingness to speak up. They will also learn concrete and reusable tools for analyzing data. Of course, the overarching thread that links the designs is that they engage the brainpower of the whole team.

Which design you end up using in any given situation will depend on your goals for the team. Each has its own strengths and limitations and will require different skills and behaviors from the participants. As you increase your confidence in facilitating these designs and understand why each approach works, you will be able to use individual parts of them, blending them together in your own way, to create unique designs.

6

BUILDING TRUST AND ENGAGEMENT

This second group of designs will provide a variety of options for building trust and increasing a team's or organization's engagement. Some of them are fun, some are arduous but rewarding, but all of them will move the team or organization forward in a meaningful way. Two of the designs (Kings, Queens, and Fairy Tales and The News Conference) can be used with teams where very little trust exists, and therefore can be applied to pretty much any group the facilitator may encounter. The other two designs (Genie in the Bottle and The 7 in 7) require teams that already have a good level of trust, so you will need to factor that in when deciding whether to employ it in a meeting.

What we do know is that when we enter an organization and ask what factors reduce its effectiveness, invariably the response most noted is the lack of trust. And when we look at what trust actually means, we most often find that there are unresolved issues of power and authority or communication, with people feeling shut down, denied information, or unappreciated. Many of the designs raised in this chapter provide strategies that could indirectly address these issues. Similarly, because trust is about process and how people work together or not, the very act of looking deeply at how we operate will positively influence process.

Again, as a reminder, take time to familiarize yourself with all the designs and their individual nuances before you decide which to use for your team. As you become more adept with the designs, you will see that all 13 are adaptable to wide-ranging situations. And most touch trust.

Kings, Queens, and Fairy Tales

Kings, Queens, and Fairy Tales is a creative design to assess problems, have some fun, and begin the problem-solving process. We all know that identifying and dealing with team and organizational dysfunctions can be dicey business, particularly as most well-intentioned organizations are conflict-averse and will choose to not deal with issues until they become almost unbearable. Our experience is that unless an organization is in the midst of a crisis, leaders will be reluctant to do anything differently. At this point, many leaders don't know what to do to get the issues on the table in a manner that doesn't increase tensions, embarrass critical players, or result in defensiveness. This design uses the power of storytelling to build trust and engagement to creatively uncover problems. It provides a means for looking at issues influencing trust in a safe and interesting manner, in which risk is minimal if leaders have a sense of humor and curiosity about their own leadership. However, if they lack a sense of humor and a willingness to look at the issues blocking the maximum performance of the team or organization, don't use this design. The assumption is that most people know such blockages exist and that when they are expressed in an open and humorous manner, it will provide relief, leading to a sense of optimism that change is possible. But, as in most situations in which serious change is needed, "ownership" of the issues is the essential first step before any positive actions can be expected. Kings, Queens, and Fairy Tales provides such ownership without blame or shame. It is a diagnostic tool that opens the door to positive solutions.

Step 1: The Setup

The Kings, Queens, and Fairy Tales design works best when you can schedule a half-day session, preferably at an off-site location. The design could be done in a large training on-site room, but the off-site location is helpful for encouraging participants to be more willing to risk doing things differently, because they are not in their usual work environment. Select a cross section of up to 25 participants from different levels within the organization: managers, supervisors and hourly paid associates, or executives, managers, and direct reports (Figure 6-1). Divide the participants into four groups of six to seven people. You can do this activity with a homogeneous group with similar roles and authority, but having a mixed group, as you will see, usually results in an exciting process with laughter, insight, and positive feelings.

Figure 6-1. The Setup

Step 1: The Setup

Select a cross section of up to 25 participants

Managers

Supervisors

Hourly Paid Associates

TOP TIP

Have two of the groups be people from the same level, and two of the groups be mixed-level personnel. Having groups of both mixed-level and same-level personnel will give you the best balance between participant risk and contrasting viewpoints. The resulting diagnostic stories will then reflect different issues that each group believes needs to be addressed.

Make sure everyone has a note pad and pen and that there are four flipchart pads on easels—one for each of the four groups. You should also gather some props to support the out-of-the-box thinking that is sure to occur, such as funny hats or scarves, tools, or utensils. Include anything that might help the groups tell their stories and get into character. The point is that creativity and fun are encouraged.

Step 2: The Creative Introduction

When the participants arrive, set the scene for the activity immediately. Acknowledge that this will be very different from what they were expecting or have ever been asked to do before. Tell the group you are a wizard and it is essential that everyone follows your directions, or you will cast a spell on them (Figure 6-2). Tell them that for this session, they are all members of some kingdom (their organization) and that there has been trouble brewing for some time. The king or queen (their CEO or organization leader) has asked you to help bring the issues out so they can be solved. They have ordered absolute honesty from this fine gathering they've chosen to help bring harmony back to the kingdom.

Figure 6-2. The Wizard

Explain that the small groups will be tasked with creating stories to depict what life is like in their kingdom, so the king or queen can really understand the issues and then do something about them. It might also be useful to create some ground rules for the group, such as no judgment, what happens in Vegas stays in Vegas, and the stories must be funny. It takes cooperation to build these stories, and the ground rules give people permission to act differently in a safe way.

TOP TIP As the facilitator, you might want to consider wearing a black cape so you can really get into the role of the wizard—and subconsciously give the participants permission to get into their roles.

Divide them into the four groups and give them one hour to create a 15-minute story about the kingdom. Have them use the language and characters of King Arthur's Middle Ages to describe life in their kingdom and the problems that exist. Tell them that in those far-off days, there were dragons and knights, wizards and princes, serfs and wenches—and they can let their imaginations go wild as they use these characters to describe the current state of their community. Show them the box of props you have prepared and tell them that they can use whatever they want to help them tell their stories and get into character.

Using the language of the times, they need to identify all the issues present that keep the current kingdom from being the best-performing kingdom anywhere. Tell them they do not have to solve the issues—just present them in their stories so they can be solved later. Before they start on their stories, have the groups spend 10 minutes writing down the unfinished business they think needs addressing. For example, there might be issues with power and authority, unclear roles, competition from rival organizations, or conflicts that people are unwilling to resolve. There might have even been a recent failure that encompasses multiple issues that they can draw from.

Now have the groups begin thinking about what kinds of stories would represent the issues without having to fix them. This kind of thinking is a stretch for even the most creative participants, so give them some examples of things they might find to help start them off (Figure 6-3). A whole example story is also a good idea; here is one really short example that we have drawn from recent world news:

> Once upon a far-off time in the kingdom of Social Mediarnia, the poor people were extremely upset at the king's decision to sell their personal details to the wicked prince. The king didn't think he was doing anything wrong when he made his decision, so he was very confused as to why his people were so upset. In an effort to make good, the king called in the Wizard of Spin to help figure out what should be done to make them all live happily ever after.

Clearly, the issues must be understandable, important, and fixable.

Tell them that in their stories, titles and people can be recognizable—who the king or queen is, who the sorcerer is, or who is the pretender to the throne—but tell them not to use anyone's names. If the participants can figure out who people are by the stories, that's fine; just don't directly name people. Encourage them to explore humor in their stories. And before the session, you may want to let the leader know that they might be the brunt of some honest humor, and how they handle it will be very important. You could also encourage the leader to tell the group that the group shouldn't hold back. If the leader can't handle the brutal truth that will be produced by this process, then don't use this design. Or, if the organization is in the midst of a crisis and there is hostility, anger, and open antagonism, there are other designs that might prove useful, such as Future Search.

Figure 6-3. Example for Participants

Step 3: The Presentations

After their hour of design time (always check in and see if the groups could use another 10 or 15 minutes prior to the end of the allocated time), gather the groups together and have them present their 15-minute stories in turn. Remind the groups before they present that honesty rules and humor and exaggeration can be used to make their points. Introduce each group by saying "Once upon a time in the Kingdom of (whatever you named it), there was some trouble, and things were not all they could be. . . ." Then encourage them to begin.

At the end of each story, ask the other three groups observing to identify the issues that need addressing. As the facilitator, write each issue they offer down on a piece of flipchart paper, but allow no discussion yet (Figure 6-4). Don't worry too much about the time each group will take to present. We find that the presentations rarely last the full 15 minutes, but we set them up with this expectation to make sure they take the activity seriously. At the end of the four stories, ask the group whether there are significant differences in the stories or the issues coming from them. If so, explore with the group what these differences are.

Step 4: The "So What"

Divide the participants into new groups by counting off by five. Give these new groups 30 minutes to agree on the top three issues that must be addressed if this Kingdom is to be the best it can be (Figure 6-5). For each issue they decide on, they must provide an argument for their choice.

Figure 6-4. Issues to Address

Figure 6-5. The "So What"

Then get the whole group back together, and take the number one issue and reason from each of the five groups. Capture each issue and reason as they are given on a piece of flipchart paper. If an issue is offered more than once, make a note on the paper to reflect this. Continue going around the group until you have everybody's top three in a prioritized list. This might also be a time to use the Las Vegas Vote design discussed previously as a means of establishing your prioritized list.

The next step after this design will be to present the prioritized list to the king or queen—that is, the CEO or managing director of the organization. A good way to do this is to select one person from each of the story groups to act as a steering committee, and have them meet with the leader to present the list and develop a plan for next steps. The steering committee will be the ones that develop the detailed plan and present it, but make sure that the prioritized issues are agreed to by the whole group before you close out the session. Once the steering committee has presented the top three issues to the leader (although they could present four or five at most), you can also ask them to verbalize the issues back to the group so they know the leader has heard them as they were intended and agrees that they need addressing.

Scanning the other designs offered, the steering committee also may suggest a design for addressing one or more of the issues, as well as a timeframe.

Here is a summary of the steps with the time needed for each.

Step 1: The Setup	30 Minutes to 1 Hour (Before the Session)
Step 2: The Creative Bit	1 Hour
Step 3: The Presentations	1 Hour
Step 4: The "So What"	1 Hour
Total Design:	**3 Hours**

Genie in the Bottle

Genie in the Bottle (Figure 6-6) is a creative design that provides a safe way to ask for and receive feedback in a group setting. It is also a useful vehicle for teaching an inexperienced group the fundamentals of good feedback.

Figure 6-6. Genie in the Bottle

When we ask ourselves what differentiates high-performing teams from groups that seriously underperform, we have one test that rarely fails us. It is a simple question: Does the group give and receive feedback regularly, skillfully, and in real time? Without regular feedback, there is no ability to course-correct, no way to evaluate performance, and no means of holding individuals or teams to particular standards. Feedback is at the heart of effective leadership and ensures opportunities for personal and organizational growth. It provides individuals, teams, and organizations information about performance and behavior that can be used to improve choices. Feedback conversations are difficult because they demand some skill in delivering feedback and readiness on the part of those receiving it. When using feedback, we must be conscious of both our reasons for doing so and the interest or willingness of those who will be receiving the feedback. What we experience, however, is that feedback in most teams and organizations remains a seriously avoided, sometimes abused, and often misunderstood aspect of leadership.

This design is meant to shine a light on feedback and provide a means of practicing giving it in a safe and interesting way. Usually the very idea of giving or receiving feedback feels challenging because more often than not, it's seen as a negative process (Figure 6-7). The Genie in the Bottle design is meant to change this association and, during the process, build feedback skills while increasing both camaraderie and trust. Feedback is, theoretically, neither negative or positive. It is descriptive information about people and their behavior as they carry out their work. It should be an accepted and natural aspect of all leadership practices.

Figure 6-7. Feedback Is Often Seen as Negative

The design is adapted from the story of Aladdin and the magic lamp. You know the one—Aladdin discovers a hidden cave and a treasure trove of gold and jewels. For some reason, he is attracted to an old lamp in the back of the cave. As he is rubbing the dust off, a genie miraculously appears, announcing, "Master, you have three wishes." And that is the beginning of many stories and jokes about what Aladdin asked for and the trouble he caused.

In this design, however, each person in the group has their own genie who will ask three questions on their behalf instead of granting wishes. The people in the room have to know one another—usually as colleagues who have observed one another in work situations—so that both knowledge and some trust are assumed and the group has sufficient willingness to participate in this process. This is important because everyone in the group will receive feedback from their peers. If you don't have these two elements, don't use this design. Choose other options from our 13 designs to first build the trust or intimacy that is lacking.

Usually we suggest a group size of at least seven participants for this activity, but it can be run with up to 40. For larger groups, individuals will give their genie the names of only 10 people to provide feedback, otherwise you could be there all week gathering responses. Our process works well because people choose from whom they wish to receive feedback. Also, everybody in the room receives the same amount of feedback, based on the same three questions. The information is then organized and analyzed by each genie and fed back to each individual in a very prescribed manner. The design ensures that people on the team all share the same risk, and nobody is going to end up with a huge "dump" of negative data. Everyone is encouraged to solicit feedback from a broad selection of people, which ensures the most honest and balanced feedback possible.

Step 1: The Setup

Divide the participants into groups of three. Each group of three will have a Person A, B, and C. Person A will be the genie for Person B, Person B the genie for Person C, and Person C the genie for Person A (Figure 6-8).

If the number of people you have does not divide equally into threes, use some pairs as well. Tell the participants that any information generated in the activity will be anonymous, and feedback shared in the groups of three stays in the groups of three. It's important that this rule of anonymity be honored. If you lack confidence in this, choose another activity.

Figure 6-8. Genies

Step 2: The Rules

In these newly formed groups of three, ask them to consider what four or five rules must be established for the giving and receiving of feedback in a manner that is respectful and safe. Give them 10 minutes to craft their lists of inviolate rules of feedback. You will then take one idea at a time from each group and post it on a flip-chart. To keep the rules from being a huge laundry list, for each idea offered, ask the rest of the group if they have anything similar and add check marks to the item you just wrote to represent these. When you pare the rules down, the list rarely ends up being more than four or five rules long (Figure 6-9). Here are a few of our favorites:

- Describe the behavior.
- Give an example of specific behavior.
- Explain how the behavior makes people feel.
- Give the feedback as close as possible to the time that it occurred.
- Use the information as a stimulus to change behavior, if the recipient chooses.

The point of this exercise is to teach the participants the skill of giving feedback and let them practice it before they go collect the data in their role of genie.

TOP TIP Having generated the list from the group at this point, tell them that describing the individual's behavior specifically with examples is key, and not to place judgments in the conversation, such as, "You are a bad person."

Figure 6-9. Feedback Rules

Remind the group that feedback is neither positive nor negative. It is just information that the receiver can accept and use or not. If a participant doesn't like the feedback, they can call it negative. There is no obligation to accept the feedback. However, if the majority of those interviewed have agreed to an issue or two, the person might want to seriously consider them. Let's say that several people tell your genie that you tend to interrupt a lot. Is that negative or positive? Of course, you can choose to be annoyed and defensive. But if you choose to see the information as helpful, you can make it positive—even see it as a gift. Similarly, the feedback that "you intimidate people" is useful only if the recipient knows the behavior that creates the feeling of intimidation in others.

General statements like "you're friendly" aren't helpful because you need to know what you do to warrant being called friendly. So, the genies should ask for an example or two. It's their job to bring their Aladdin useful information. Specific, descriptive behaviors tend to keep those pesky judgments out. The point of the genie is to provide people with choices they can use to increase their effectiveness.

Step 3: The Questions

The newly formed groups of three give each other the names of seven to 10 people from whom they would like to receive feedback. If you have a very small group (fewer than 12), there is no need to nominate whom they want to receive feedback from; just ask everybody. Quality responses with useful examples is the key.

The participants are then given the following three questions:

1. What are *X*'s three greatest strengths they bring to the team, or the job? Please be specific.
2. What are *X*'s three areas of improvement that would help them become an even more effective leader or team member? Again, please be specific.
3. What are two things *X* needs to be told but, for whatever reason, people might be reluctant to tell them? (We assume that people want to know the answer even if it is uncomfortable.)

Step 4: The Genie

Suggest to the group that genies separate one page in their notebooks for each question. This makes it easier to organize the data later. Then, give them one hour to go around the room and interview each person on their list with all three questions (Figure 6-10). Again, encourage specific and descriptive examples. With lots of people seeking information, it's likely that some individuals will be more sought-out than others. Therefore, it's important to stay focused on the three questions and keep moving. About five minutes per person works best to ensure the design does not create problems around time. Initially, with lots of people seeking individuals to ask questions, it may feel a bit chaotic. But that is part of the fun, and soon people will sense a certain rhythm to the process.

Figure 6-10. Genies Asking Questions

Step 4: The Genie Bit

Then take one hour to go around the room and do your interviews

Step 5: Organizing the Data

After the hour of interviews, the genies go off by themselves to organize their data. (Again, check how the group is doing. If after 40 to 50 minutes you sense most people need additional time, let the group know that you are adding an additional 10 minutes.) We use our process of truths, trends, and unique ideas to organize the data and to feed the information back to each Aladdin. It is a process that we often combine with other designs, such as Future Search, 6-Step Problem Solving, or The Carousel. If you have already learned this process from using another one of our 13 designs, you can skip this part of the text.

Truths: A truth is a statement made repeatedly by those interviewed. It may include 50 percent of those responding or more. It's such a consistent piece of information that it leaps off the page, simply cannot be denied, and must be heard by the person. Among the three questions there may be one, two, or many truths. Usually there are some. Occasionally, the responses from questions two and three are similar and together they add up to a truth. Also, in looking at the person's strengths, it is often useful to see if some of their areas of needed development could be the result of overusing a strength—a common and interesting insight. For example, a very friendly person might be averse to conflict, because if they engaged in conflict they might be seen as not so friendly.

Trends: A trend is information that does not appear as frequently as a truth but needs to be recognized. If a person interviews 10 people and three or four suggested the same thing, it would be categorized as a trend rather than a truth.

Unique Ideas: Often individuals being interviewed have a different perspective, an insight that the genie believes should not be lost. There won't be many, but two or three creative ideas may be seen as important to share. This is the genie's call as to whether they believe the information will be valuable to the receiver.

Step 6: The Feedback

This is the time when the groups of three get back together and begin sharing their data. A gives B feedback, B gives C feedback, and so on (Figure 6-11).

It is also the time to listen carefully to the information being provided, with the person receiving feedback asking questions for clarification. If A is giving B feedback, C also listens carefully because occasionally they may have something to add, such as a new insight or another example. This is B's time to ask clarifying questions—not the time to try to fix things. In this instance, A's job is to frame the feedback and offer it in a way that B can hear. The goal is for B to hear the information and to explore it with the other two people. Talking about how the information feels to B is also part of the equation. Because this is strictly information sharing, each person takes only about 15 minutes before moving on to the next person. Again, there will be time for problem solving later—this time is purely for clarifying the data from the interviews. It is a time to gain understanding in relation to the feedback they just received. Note that this design is diagnostic in nature and should not be used to solve issues. Instead, use the 6-Step Problem Solving design or another model at a later time.

Figure 6-11. Genies Giving Feedback

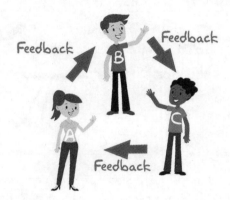

Step 7: The Wrap-Up

After all the groups have shared their information, a closing circle of all the participants occurs. Here it is useful to go around and ask how each person feels about their data and the process, and have them share one fact or insight they are taking from the experience.

TOP TIP

Make sure this final go-around is affirming. Some people may report a piece of feedback that makes them feel bad. Have them put a positive spin on it by asking, "So how can that be helpful?" Or ask to hear one of their more positive pieces of feedback.

If additional time is available after completing the activity, it is often helpful to move straight into the 6-Step Problem Solving design as a follow-up. Here, each person would take an issue—a piece of data from their feedback—and dive into it, with the goal of bringing greater insight to the information and developing strategies for improvement (Figure 6-12). If there is no time, it can be useful for the three-person groups to meet on their own to complete the 6-Step Problem Solving design. We suggest this because it is rare to have such an experience with individuals you now trust.

Figure 6-12. Working With the Feedback

Once the Genie in the Bottle design has been completed, participants can share the insights gained with their leaders as part of their regular supervisory or appraisal process. It's a perfect opportunity to build support and develop greater trust in these relationships.

A word of caution: In our conflict-averse society, where feedback is often not a meaningful part of workplace culture, individuals can go years without receiving useful feedback. For some, even though they may want it, it can be very difficult to receive. Participants in this process ought to be involved in some kind of follow-up with a supervisor or with the group that they worked with during the design. Key questions to be considered during the follow-up would be how they feel about the feedback they received and what they are planning to do with it.

SCALING THE DESIGN

In this example, we used a group of eight, which gave us two subgroups of three and a pair. If we had 40 members, this would result in 12 groups of three and two pairs. Try to have as many groups of three as possible, and then use pairs to make the math work.

Here is a summary of the seven easy steps with the time needed for each.

Step 1: The Setup	10 Minutes
Step 2: The Rules	15 Minutes
Step 3: The Questions	5 Minutes
Step 4: The Genie	60-90 Minutes
Step 5: Organizing the Data	30-45 Minutes
Step 6: The Feedback	45 Minutes
Step 7: The Wrap-Up	15 Minutes
Total Design:	**3-4 Hours***

*(*depending on the number of participants)*

The 7 in 7

The 7 in 7 design (Figure 6-13) is an excellent way to build increased trust and stronger relationships within a team. It is a fairly delicate design to execute, because the focus is on sharing personal information, and it depends on the facilitator's deep belief in the process and their sincere modeling of it during the instruction phase. To make the participants feel safe, the facilitator has to lead from the heart and provide meaningful modeling. It is therefore a slightly different design from the others, requiring more attention to the readiness of the team and sincere support from both the facilitator and the leader. However, if you and the group have this willingness to dig deep and take a risk, the group will never be the same again.

Figure 6-13. The 7 in 7

Already have a good level of trust between them

Design 8: The 7 in 7

Let's take a closer look at what drives this design. Undertaking a deep dive into yourself is, for many of us, breaking all the rules. It is not something that everyone feels comfortable doing—digging into how we're perceived, pulling off the covers of our family of origin to see what really makes us tick. But these parts of us determine the kind of baggage we carry around, which is often detrimental to our behavior. And, while we may be aware to some degree of our impact, it is rare that we have the opportunity to learn from others and their stories. One thing is true, however: We all have stories. We also have secrets that few ever know and that can keep us limited in our ability to communicate, lead, or be a positive team member.

Let's imagine that most of us believe that we should be the best we possibly can be, live a productive life, and not hold ourselves back from our potential. To do that means we have to know as much about ourselves as possible. Such an exploration is bound to uncover areas of strength as well as deficiencies. Before moving toward a better self, you have to own your deficiencies. One way to do this is to share what you learn with a friend, or even a team of people you really trust or would like to trust.

When you can share your strengths and limitations, you take a major step toward owning your imperfect self, and it frees you to try on new ideas and behaviors. But to even get a glimpse of the possibilities open to you, you have to be vulnerable. And that is not in most of our plans for life (Figure 6-14). It is much easier to remain comfortable, to not invite risk by exposing our weaknesses, than to have the courage to open that door of conversation.

One thing we have learned over the years of using this design is that if we are willing to engage in some shared risk with individuals we trust, we are then more

Figure 6-14. Vulnerability Is Difficult

willing to take even greater risks by looking at what holds us back. Therefore, feeling support and care from others is an avenue toward building even more honesty in our lives. Another thing we have learned is that one of the things most people want more than anything is to be accepted for who they are. We leverage this fact within the 7 in 7 design to help encourage people to share deeply with one another.

The power behind this design comes from creating an opportunity for people to share their information with others who are also willing to be vulnerable, who will therefore not judge anybody and their limitations. What stops us from living this way is that we don't have the time required to build the trust necessary to share this openly. Most of us are lucky to have one or two people in our lives with whom we can be so open and vulnerable—and these people are not usually our teammates at work. This design helps create that trust safely and rapidly (Figure 6-15).

Some people will inevitably pull us aside and say, "I didn't come here for therapy." Our response goes something like, "Well, life is all about therapy. Changing ourselves and helping others to be the best we can be, whether at home or work, is what enriches our personal stories and provides us with new and valuable choices." Same old, same old will not provide the key to that lock.

Figure 6-15. Creating Trust

This design is meant for intact teams of three or more people who already have a basic level of trust among them, or at the very least an open understanding of one another and are seeking to take this to the next level. Please again note: This design will not be effective unless some trust exists within the team already and there is interest in going deep.

The premise of the design is simple. Each member of the participating team is asked to go off by themselves and generate a list of the seven most powerful events or relations that have shaped who they are as an individual today. These can be either positive or negative experiences (Figure 6-16).

Figure 6-16. Generate a List of Powerful Experiences

The idea is that unless the group knows these critical parts of who they are as individuals, they cannot truly know themselves and what makes them tick. Being willing to risk sharing these facts creates a bonding experience. Often the list includes stories about families and the consequence of parental or sibling relationships, a traumatic event that changed how someone acts or feels, or a teacher or mentor who changed them forever. What is essential is that they have left an indelible imprint on how the person thinks, acts, and what they deeply believe. These events are core to who we are—and who we are still becoming. Most of us have more than seven and will experience others as we continue to develop.

Step 1: The Setup

Preparing a group of individuals to share intimate, powerful facts about who they are demands the facilitator take a personal approach. They must communicate a deep belief in the value of the activity and be willing to model the process. If the facilitator is not willing to demonstrate a high level of risk and hence trust, then who are they to ask the same of the group? Thus, the facilitator must first explain what the design is about and why it is important (Figure 6-17). The goal here is to convey to the group that this activity increases trust toward one another, and will help them become a more productive, cohesive team.

Figure 6-17. Facilitator Must Explain the Activity's Importance

The facilitator must first explain what the design is about – and why it is important

The goal is to convey to the group that this activity will allow them to:

- ✓ Increase trust.
- ✓ Become a more cohesive team.
- ✓ Be more productive.

Step 2: The Modeling

The facilitator must model an example or two from their life so that the group really begins to know who they are as a person. The most important thing about this step is that they must set a high bar for the group. It's not necessary to share all seven experiences during the introduction, unless the facilitator is a critical member of the team. If this is the case, the facilitator should introduce the activity with a personal example or two, but then share the rest later. Sharing that they were born on a rainy night in Omaha is not a high bar.

Here are a couple of examples to help the facilitator identify suitably deep experiences for the modeling:

1. They might have been abused as a child by an alcoholic father and left home at an early age to avoid further abuse, resulting in a mistrust of people in positions of authority.

2. Perhaps they had a mentor in college who turned their natural skepticism into optimism, motivating them to study, and eventually resulting in scholarships for further study.

3. They might have had an experience in the military or in a failed relationship that reshaped how they acted in the future.

The key here is to choose the deepest, most meaningful stories you can for the modeling. The deeper the facilitator is willing to dig, the more the group will be willing to follow them. Most likely this is new behavior for the facilitator as well. Their behavior helps define the new boundaries for the group and provides unstated permission.

Step 3: The Digging

Ask the group to take about 20 minutes to write down their seven positive or negative experiences that have profoundly shaped who they are today. These do not need to be scripted at all, just jotted down as reminders of what to talk about next. Sharing should feel like a conversation with friends and not at all contrived.

Step 4: The Sharing

Using what you know about the group, you need to select the first person who will share their story. Above all, this needs to be someone who will risk being totally authentic for the rest of the group (Figure 6-18). It is not a great idea, usually, to have the leader go first. Better to wait a round or two until they and the group are ready for them to share. As facilitator, you must have a sense of how open the leader can be. Unless you know the leader well and this person has a good, open relationship with their group, this can lead to the sharing being at a rather awkward and shallow level. Asking for volunteers to go first who can encourage people to dig deeply and be great role models for the group is often a much safer way to kick this process off. However, because the sharing step will occur only after some time, the facilitator will see evidence that will determine

Figure 6-18. Choosing the First Person to Share

their choice of a candidate to go first. Thus, once you have observed even a brand-new group for a little while as facilitator, you can generally pick out the individuals who are likely to be willing to share first, and then encourage them to go for it. But whomever you choose, the first person must be willing to model the necessary openness.

Before the first person shares their story, tell the group that they will be expected to generate one or two questions at the end of the story for the person doing the sharing. This participation helps to create a shared experience and provides support for the person sharing. This also reduces the possible awkwardness and sense of isolation that can follow such meaningful sharing. The questions can add more depth and show that the listeners care. And it's safe to assume that some people, as they hear the stories of their teammates, will add more risk and substance to their own stories when it's their turn.

The facilitator will also choose the second person to share their story, again someone they believe will model openness. Try to take time to prepare the second person up front, the same way you did the first. Once the first two stories have been shared, a high level of candor will usually have been established and going forward, you can request volunteers from the group (Figure 6-19).

It is the facilitator's decision how many stories should be shared at one time, but it is unusual for two individuals to share in a row, because the involvement and emotion generated can be exhausting. A good idea is to insert a different kind of activity to bolster energy in between each 7 in 7 sharing (Figure 6-20). These are best done one at a time, with a couple of hours in between each one, and over several different days. If you need to do two in a row, give the group a 10-minute break between each 7 in 7 sharing.

TOP TIP Be sure to let whomever you choose to go first know what you will be asking of them in advance so they can ready themselves. Tell them the reason they are being chosen is that you know they will do a great job of sharing deeply and modeling for the rest of the group. Such support needs to be authentic.

Figure 6-19. Request Volunteers After the First Two Stories

Figure 6-20. Schedule Activities in Between Sharing

The design's name comes from our original intention of sharing seven stories in seven minutes. We discovered, though, that the sharing takes more like 20 or 30 minutes per person, especially when you factor in questions from the group. When the sessions take this long, you know you have them at a deep enough level.

Step 5: The "So What"

After several people have shared their stories, at some point take time to process the event. Ask these types of questions of the group: "What have you experienced so far? What did you learn? What is the value of the design?" You can use this feedback to determine whether the process should continue, or how to space out the stories. The true readiness of the group you are working with can only be determined by how the participants respond to the task. Our experience is that most participants feel it is scary, but also exciting and enlightening. The discussion often generates confidence in some members who have been holding back, even though they may wish to jump in.

Here is a summary of the steps with the time needed for each.

Step 1: The Setup	20 Minutes
Step 2: The Modeling	10 Minutes
Step 3: The Digging	20 Minutes
Step 4: The Sharing	20-30 Minutes per Person
Step 5: The "So What"	10 Minutes
Total Design:	**90 Minutes***

(*for the first person, then 30 minutes per person in the group over several days)

Real-Life Example of 7 in 7

Some years ago, we were working with a new team of senior executives from a highly competitive, take-no-prisoners type of organization. The members of the team had suggested that their climb to the top of the billion-dollar company had taken a huge toll on their trust, their work relationships, and their sense of who they were as human beings. In our pre-interviews with the 10 individuals, they had all indicated that they hoped this team would be open and supportive versus competitive and aggressive. While we were skeptical, we said we'd be able to tell how willing they actually were to challenge the negative norms that supported cliques: talking behind their colleagues' backs, not disclosing many ideas and feelings, avoiding efforts at cooperative conflict resolution, or not bringing their disagreements directly to the individuals with whom they differed. This would signify a major shift in their team culture and would challenge the very behaviors that had made them successful.

After lunch one day, we asked them to each go off by themselves for a few minutes and identify the seven most powerful experiences in their lives that had made them the person they are today. If we didn't know these things, we couldn't possibly really "know" them. On the surface, no big deal. But, the task threw most of them into a quandary. How honest could they—or would they—be? They knew that many of their work experiences had damaged them, or they might be ones that they were not proud of but, indeed, had shaped who they were. Some would be drawn from their family history and powerful people in their lives, some from failures or successes, and some from positive models. This was to be an opportunity for each to share deeply and personally. As examples, we shared two of our own. We also explained that this was to be their first opportunity to build the trust they said they wanted, and to demonstrate that they could alter the nature of their relationships as well as their commitments to each other.

We chose two individuals who had previously demonstrated they were open and would probably relish the opportunity to share their stories. They set a high bar for the others; you could almost feel some of the other members adding more challenging parts to their own stories as they listened to the compelling accounts of what made these individuals who they were. The team realized that superficial stories would not meet the standard set by their two colleagues.

One shared about his violent family. He eventually ran away from home at 17, to get away from the insanity. There were audible gasps as individuals began to understand who he was and the burden he still carried. At the end of each story, the other members were to ask an additional question. Again, our belief was that such sharing would leave many of the team members feeling vulnerable, and questions from the group would bring some normalcy to a very abnormal situation.

That group would never be the same. Because they shared at such a profound level, there was little that they would not share in the way of ideas and feelings in the future. Experiencing their team members being so authentic also revealed how superficial they often were with each other and in their lives generally. Their world of work had changed to include more humor, greater compassion, greater candor, and the willingness to provide feedback about almost anything.

So, much of the 7 in 7's success depends on the facilitator's belief in the process and their willingness to model the candor required. Authentic behavior provides the essential openness for this design to succeed. There is no script, because sincerity comes from the heart and not the head. But, if the team leader does not actively support the process, it will not succeed.

The News Conference

The News Conference (Figure 6-21) is a design for getting the truth on the table. If you ask any leader how open and transparent they are, they will most likely answer that they speak the truth and that people in their organization are also free to speak their truth without fear of recrimination or negative consequences. People say they want the truth, but sometimes it is hard to get the truth out. And because the whole truth is so seldom shared with those in power, it can also be a shock when it is finally heard. Also, if you ask whether any participants have ever withheld difficult information that ought to have been shared but they lacked the courage to do so, the answer is almost unanimously yes.

Figure 6-21. News Conference

Design 9: The News Conference

- Tear down barriers
- Bring the unsaid into the open
- Create greater trust

The News Conference design is a really simple way of drawing the truth out from participants who normally keep their mouths shut and their ideas to themselves. Using it can tear down barriers, bring the unsaid into the open, and create greater trust between leadership and employees.

Step 1: The Setup

Have the leader and their team tell those present that they wish to be transparent and to really understand peoples' concerns no matter what. Have them make sure the participants understand that they do want the truth, and this might be a stretch for both sides. Basically, they are asking for help, and they have to make it safe for people to help them (Figure 6-22).

Step 2: The Information Gathering

Hand out three cue cards to every participant and tell them to write down on each one a tough, challenging question. These can be about the leader or the management team, the organization or how it operates. Tell them again not to hold back.

Figure 6-22. The Setup

Step 1: The Setup

Leadership Team   Leader

We wish to understand people's concerns – no matter what these might be

We really DO want the truth !! And we know this might be a stretch for all of us

We need your help !

TOP TIP Let people know that these questions will be anonymously posed before they write them down. This will ensure that people will not hold back in asking the most challenging and meaningful questions possible.

Step 3: The Prioritization

Let's imagine a five-person executive team and 20 members of the next level of management, all of whom report to a member of the executive team.

Now divide the larger group into four or five small groups, perhaps randomly counting off by numbers so friendship or work groups are split (Figure 6-23). Give the small groups 15 minutes to choose the four most powerful questions from their collective ideas that they all agree need to be asked. What they'll soon realize is that behind every question is an implied statement about the leader of the team or organization.

While the small groups are working, spend a few minutes with the leader and management team, quietly persuading them to not be defensive about the questions when they are eventually posed. The more you can have them model openness to hearing the truth, the more people are likely to give it. Because you will allow two follow-up questions for each question, the candor of *those* questions is determined by the perceived openness and curiosity of the leader.

Figure 6-23. The Prioritization

Step 4: The Shuffle

Now gather the top four cards from each of the four groups, shuffle them up in front of everyone, and redistribute the cards among the small groups. Each group will once again have four cards, but they could have come from anywhere in the room. There is no way the leader can know from where the question comes, but they do know that at least three other people (the others in the small group) agree that it is important.

Step 5: The Conference

For this next part, you need a person who is perceived as neutral; thus, the facilitator goes to each group in turn and asks them to read out one of their cards. The leader can answer, as can any of the other management team members at the front of the room. However, limit the total time to five minutes per card. People from the floor can ask a follow-up question for greater clarity, but limit these to no more than two per card. Then go to the next group and ask them to read one of their cards. The facilitator should watch the time and be certain the leader and the rest of the group understand the question being read.

Encourage the management team to limit their defensiveness by whatever means you can. And keep going until all the cards have been read. Remember, as in many designs, this is primarily a diagnostic, attempting to get the hidden truths on the table for later problem solving. In some instances, the answers are evident, but the norms of the organization can contribute to a culture of denial, fear, or lack of will to face the truth.

In short, this design is a diagnostic exercise to provide the leaders with the concerns and tough questions that people believe need to be addressed. It is almost certain that you will need other activities after this one to generate solutions to many of the issues raised. But this design is a great start to the process.

Here are some real questions that were raised while we facilitated this design:

- Why have we not addressed the conflicts between production and distribution?
- Would you please explain our apparent loss of market share raised in your report today?
- What two problems keep you (the CEO) awake at night and why?
- To the CIO: What are you doing to curb what some say is an anger management problem between you and some others at your level?
- What is behind the upswing in safety-related problems?

Here is a summary of the steps with the time needed for each.

Step 1: The Setup	5 Minutes
Step 2: The Information Gathering	5 Minutes
Step 3: The Prioritization	15 Minutes
Step 4: The Shuffle	5 Minutes
Step 3: The Conference	60-90 Minutes
Total Design:	**2 Hours**

(Note: Some leaders like to have a wine and beer session after the News Conference for 20 or 30 minutes, to relax the situation. This is optional.)

This chapter demonstrated four designs that can build trust and increase engagement. They all have common threads. For example, these designs will also help with developing the skill of active listening. The very act of experiencing them will improve the team's communication skills and willingness to speak up. These designs can also be used for creatively solving problems. Again, the overarching thread that links all our designs is that they engage the brainpower of the whole team. Success depends on input and some mutual risk taking from many of those involved.

What are your goals for the team you're working with? What new skills and behaviors do you want to leave them with? Use these questions to help you decide which design to use, or what parts of them you can blend to create your own designs.

7

DEALING WITH CONFLICT

This final group of designs will provide a variety of tools for dealing with individual or team conflict. In conflict situations, trust is compromised in some way. These designs therefore require very little trust from the participants. In fact, two of the designs can be used in situations where zero trust exists. The other two designs require teams that have some low level of trust, so they can be used in most situations.

Conflict can sometimes arise unexpectedly, so two of our designs can be run as emergencies—where the facilitator decides in the moment that there is conflict that needs to be dealt with. They require no preparation and can be done in as little as 30 minutes.

Again, take time to familiarize yourself with all the designs and their individual nuances before you decide which to use for your team.

The 8 and 6

The 8 and 6 (Figure 7-1) is a powerful design for resolving conflict between two people, while at the same time building a more positive and constructive relationship between them. It works because it engages the participants in a highly structured process that ensures equal risk.

Figure 7-1. The 8 and 6

Design 10: The 8 and 6

There are a couple of assumptions that need to be satisfied before choosing this design. First, the two conflicting parties need to be committed to resolving the conflict. This could be because they believe their current situation must change, or because they have been told to fix it or else. Second, the third-party facilitator (you) is trusted by both individuals to at least be a fair referee in the process.

Step 1: The Setup

Schedule at least a half day for this design in a neutral, off-site location. If an off-site location isn't possible, make sure to choose a soundproof office location that doesn't indicate a preference for one individual over the other, or doesn't have windows through which people can be seen. Some people want instant resolution and see a half day spent with people in conflict as rather onerous. If this happens, you might want to point out to them the cost to the team or organization in terms of productivity and morale if the conflict were to continue, and how their conflict bleeds into other relationships and functions.

You'll need to prepare a notebook and pen for each of the two people, some large sheets of flipchart paper, two easels, markers, and masking tape. Set up the room with the easels facing away from each other (Figure 7-2). This is just to give the two people some privacy for writing.

Step 2: The Information Gathering

Initially tell the two people that they will each be stationed at their own easel

Figure 7-2. The Setup

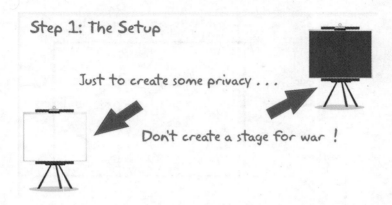

Step 1: The Setup

Just to create some privacy . . .

Don't create a stage for war !

containing flipchart paper. When they get to their easels, ask them to split the top sheet into three equal parts by drawing two vertical lines on the page. Then ask them to label the left and right columns with "My Strengths" and "They Will Say," respectively (Figure 7-3).

Explain that the left column should contain their own eight greatest behavioral strengths as a person, leader, or team member. The right column should contain what they believe the other person will say are their eight greatest strengths. The rule is that each person must write eight items in each column and be able to provide a behavioral example of each strength. This means an example of something that they do that demonstrates the strength, which other people can observe. The assumption is that even enemies or those in conflict have many strengths, or they wouldn't be working in the organization.

Once they finish this task, ask them to write in their notebooks the other person's eight greatest strengths. It is important to make sure the participants each write eight things even if they seem incapable of listing this many. Much of the time the underlying reason for any resistance is that the conflict they are trying to resolve has them stuck in the other person being wrong, and they cannot think of anything

TOP TIP Set the tone of the meeting by saying something like, "We will not be talking about history." This will ensure that you avoid getting into a "he said, she said" blaming discussion that would further polarize the combatants and be nearly impossible to facilitate.

Figure 7-3. Strengths

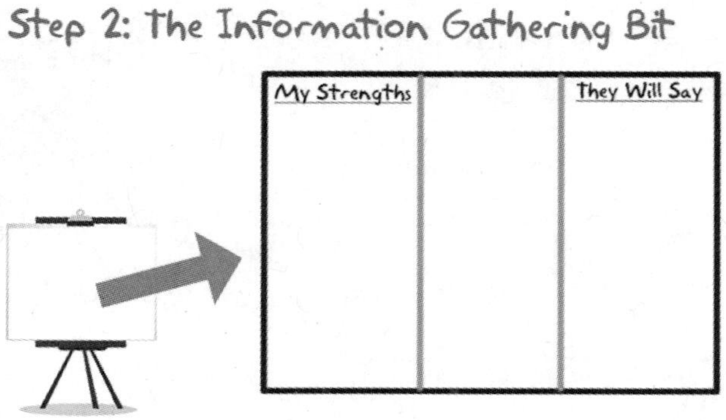

Step 2: The Information Gathering Bit

My Strengths		They Will Say

good to say about them. Forcing them to list all eight provides a means of beginning to break down these entrenched feelings, without which the conflict will never be resolved. If you work with somebody, you should be able to find at least eight good things to say about them—even if some ideas are a bit lame. As facilitator, you can also encourage the participant to think of the other person outside of work, such as saying they're a great parent. But, the key is that they must believe this is true.

Step 3: The Strength Sharing

Ask the two people to fold over their sheets as shown in Figure 7-4, then bring their easels to the middle of the room. These folds cover the text on each end of the sheets and leave the blank center column visible. Now ask for a volunteer to go first. If nobody volunteers, choose one. Because there is often a power difference between the two people, we'll usually have the subordinate person go first in giving strength-based feedback. Then, later, when they give feedback on areas of development, we have them go second, reducing the stress on the person with less authority.

TOP TIP If one of the people is the boss, have the subordinate first give the boss feedback on their strengths. When focusing on areas of development, have the boss give their areas of development first. We're assuming it's easier to receive feedback from the boss than to give it to them.

Figure 7-4. Paper Folds

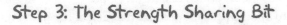

Step 3: The Strength Sharing Bit

My Strengths	They Will Say
1. Wise	1. Talker
2. Good looking	2. Smart
3. Smart	3. Good leader
4. Good leader	4. Patient
5. Patient	5. Public Speaker
6. Listener	6. Fair
7. Humble	7. Driver
8. Fair	8. Team player

Ask the person going first to stand next to their easel, while you and the other person sit down in a chair in front of them. Ask the person now sitting next to you to read out the other person's strengths one at a time, from their notebook. As they do this, the person standing will write these strengths down in the empty center column of their sheet (Figure 7-5). Remember, each piece of feedback should be accompanied with at least one specific example. The person receiving the feedback can ask clarifying questions, but cannot disagree with the information being provided.

It's critical that the person providing the feedback be able to give an example or two of each strength as they are reading them out. The facilitator is also expected

Figure 7-5. Filling in the Center Column: Strengths

to add their own examples as needed to the growing list of behavioral strengths. When we are in conflict, adversaries rarely focus on each other's strengths, so this can be somewhat uncomfortable as well as enlightening.

The next stage is to ask the person to unfold their left column and reveal their assessment of their own strengths. They present their eight items one by one, again giving examples for each. Then, they unfold their right column to reveal what they thought the other person—their adversary—would say (Figure 7-6).

Figure 7-6. Revealing Left and Right Columns

Suddenly there's a lot of information; the facilitator should explore agreements and discrepancies and encourage a good discussion about them. Try to limit any talk about overusing strengths at this point; this will be discussed later when areas of development are explored. The goal here is to have the two people recognize that there's more to the situation than a trail of negatives by first building a full picture of each other's strengths. It is usually remarkable how much agreement there is between the strengths recognized by the individual and those from the individual providing the feedback. There can be some differences when it comes to what the receiver thinks the other will say, because the conflict itself can influence how the person thinks they are seen by the other.

The process so far will often take more than an hour to complete, so after a 10-minute break, the second person stands before their easel and the same process occurs, focusing first on feedback from the other person, then comparing that with the individual's view of their strengths, and finally looking together at what the second individual thought would be said. The analysis of similarities and differences often leads to laughter and surprise, which can greatly lighten the mood between two adversaries.

Step 4: The Development

Now ask the two people to return to their easels. Once there, they divide a second sheet of flipchart paper into three columns, this time focusing on areas for development. The left column will contain what the individual believes are the six areas of development needed for them to become a more effective leader, colleague, or team member. The right column will reflect what they believe the other individual will identify as their six areas of needed development (Figure 7-7). And finally, they should write in their notebooks the development areas they see for the other person.

Figure 7-7. Areas for Development

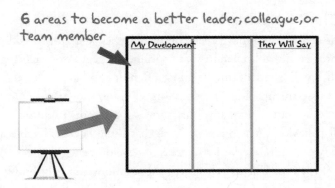

Once they're finished, repeat the process of having each one stand next to their easel, while you and the other person sit in front of them. The person sitting next to you reads out the other person's areas for development from their notebook. The person standing will write them down in the center column of their sheet (Figure 7-8).

Go through the sharing process once again with both people. At the end, explore the agreements and discrepancies and encourage a good discussion about them. As mentioned previously, often problems between two people are generated by one individual "overusing" their strengths. For example, an assertive person can become aggressive, even tyrannical, and because people don't want to take them on, over time this behavior is reinforced and becomes negative. Most of us have overused strengths in our repertoires. The facilitator must help people understand this.

Figure 7-8. Filling in the Center Column: Areas for Development

Step 5: The "So What"

Now that the analysis steps have been completed, the facilitator should work with the conflicting parties to generate some specific strategies for change. The root of the conflict will often be in the most offending behaviors identified in the eight and six assessments, and its resolution will be in how the two can support each other as allies rather than adversaries in their attempts to diminish these less than helpful behaviors. It is often the case that there is considerable agreement between the two parties in relation to areas of development (Figure 7-9).

It helps if the boss will actively accept the solutions and help both people live with the agreements made. To this end, sometimes we bring the boss of the two people in to participate in the analysis and add their views. This works well if you need the boss to hold people accountable for the details of the changes. But this could make it hard to get to the core of the conflict, especially if the boss is biased.

People are generally truthful in the first round of feedback (the eight strengths) because there is little conflict in doing so. There is often considerable similarity

TOP TIP Sometimes the person receiving the feedback will become defensive and maybe even argumentative. You can stop this by asking them to hold onto their opinions until you have seen all the items from both sides. But, it is your job as facilitator to act as the referee and not allow disagreement, because feedback is simply neutral information to be considered.

Figure 7-9. The Root of the Conflict

...and its resolution is in how the 2 can support each other as allies

and agreement between them, which is both surprising to the two adversaries and gratifying to the facilitator.

Our process leads individuals to be more candid about their own limitations for the second round (the six areas for development), because people do not want to be seen as lacking in courage about owning their weaknesses. The result is that when each looks at the other's information, there are many areas of agreement. For example, if one person sees himself as sometimes being aggressive, he will likely find that the other person agrees. There is agreement on the problem (aggression), and that leads to the possibility of a mutual solution being developed.

This process also forces the behaviors identified as areas for development to be really specific, and this means that the potential solutions will also be specific. More often than not, the former adversaries decide together how to help each other be more effective, because both realize that their own success is being blocked by the behaviors they together identified and agreed on. Accountability to each other and possibly their boss makes the change real. The boss also has the authority to suggest that they expect positive changes to occur because the current situation is not acceptable. Thus, while the two participants usually, as part of their agreed strategy, meet to discuss their progress, the facilitator can continue meeting with them periodically over the next several months to support their commitment to change.

It is also possible for each participant to take an area of development and, with the help of their partner, undertake a 6-Step Problem Solving design, helping their partner in their analysis and eventual strategies.

Here is a summary of the steps with the timing for each.

Step 1: The Setup	15 Minutes (Before the Session)
Step 2: The Information Gathering	30 Minutes
Step 3: The Strength Sharing	60 Minutes
Step 4: The Development	60 Minutes
Step 5: The "So What"	30 Minutes
Total Design:	**3 Hours**

Paradox

Paradox (Figure 7-10) is a design used to train a working group in the use of paradoxical and creative thinking to look at problems in new, fresh ways. You're doing what appears to be the opposite of what you intended to achieve your particular goal. It might sound strange, but this tactic can be very useful when you are trying to change a person's predictable response to break a repeated behavior loop. This design can help a team generate new approaches to solving habitual behavioral problems with individuals or with the team itself.

It works because human beings like to function in habitual ways. Just as we can predict another person's response to a given situation, we can also respond predictably to another's behavior. Often when we are in conflict, this results in habitual responses on both sides and the same dissatisfied feelings over and over again. It can leave people feeling unheard or misunderstood. The good news is that we can use paradox to change both our response and other people's responses.

Figure 7-10. Paradox

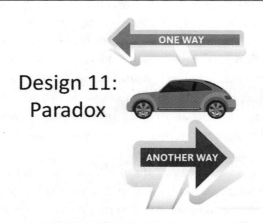

Step 1: The Setup

This design doesn't need any physical setup; the only thing you will need to do is make sure the participants understand a few assumptions and have a basic grasp of paradoxical thinking. Let's take an example of a team with 15 people. Divide them randomly into three groups of four and one group of three (Figure 7-11). These small groups will ensure a high level of participation.

Figure 7-11. The Setup

These small groups will ensure a high level of participation

First, outline the following assumptions for the group to guide them in their thinking:

1. Any solution offered should not be seen as a punishment. This means you have to think about how the solution will be received and the consequences for the parties involved.

2. You're talking about behavior, not about personality traits that cannot be changed. This is not therapy, simply a strategy for solving a perceived problem about how someone acts in predictable, often annoying, ways.

3. You are attempting to influence a behavior that may be part of a larger problem. Removal of the symptom—the repetitive, annoying, or dysfunctional behavior—is our goal, not fixing any larger problems that might exist. For example, someone may interrupt people. That would be the behavior, not the fact that the individual came from a family of

individuals who never listened to them. Our goal is not to feel helpless in the face of such behavior.

4. Consider that often the problem is in our solution—that is, our response to the other person's predictable behavior. Thus, if an individual is perpetually late and our response is to wait and be late with them as we boil inside, then the paradox to our waiting would be to leave and deal with a new reality (after a warning or two). Often we are so busy blaming the individual or being angry or annoyed that we fail to see other possible responses.

Now give the four chosen groups an example of paradox in action (Figure 7-12; you may change the details to fit your particular situation):

My husband leaves his clothes on the bedroom floor and I resent picking them up—but, predictably, I pick them up and end up nagging him. The paradox would be not to pick them up for a month and perhaps nicely suggest that we need to both be responsible for our own clothes. The problem will be whether I can stand the mess until my husband comes around to understanding. A nonparadoxical, but creative, response would be to let him know that all clothes found on the floor will cost him: $5 for socks, $10 for a shirt, and $8 for underwear. Again, the problem is often in our predictable solution to the problem. Picking the clothes up with no consequence was clearly my problem. Being willing to change my own behavior can solve the problem and also influence the other person.

Or there's the story of eight-year-old Billy and his parents. They both work, so the one way they have family time is to all go shopping together on Saturdays. One day on returning home from shopping, the parents were putting away groceries and the father smelled something burning. He rushed into the living room and saw Billy lighting the drapes on fire. He yelled and scolded Billy, but this didn't help; Billy lit four more fires in the next two weeks.

A therapist suggested that they paint a large metal oil barrel and put it at the end of his bed. Then every night for two weeks they were to build a small fire in it, sometimes singing campfire songs, roasting marshmallows, or telling stories.

After the fourth night, Billy said he didn't want to do that anymore, but the parents told him they were having such a good time that they wanted to keep it up. By the sixth evening, Billy was hiding under a pillow at the other end of the bed.

Billy's fire-setting was a symptom of the real issue. The therapist suggested that Billy simply wanted more attention, more fun with his family. The parents' solution to not having enough time for Billy was to use shopping as his fun time, and this became the problem. It was an easy fix for the parents (combining doing the chores with spending time with Billy) but that left Billy feeling left out and not cared for. A little creativity solved the problem once the parents recognized that their actions were causing it.

Figure 7-12. Example Paradox

Step 2: The Directions

In the four small groups, have the participants share a number of situations they have with anyone at work or at home that drive them crazy. It should be aggravating, behaviorally defined, and predictable. Make sure they outline the following in their discussion:

1. What does the individual do (their behavior) that is predictable and annoying?
2. What is your and others' response to the behavior? (predictable as well)
3. What is the outcome or consequence that is not helpful?
4. What is the specific behavior in the other that needs to change?
5. How does your behavior in response to the person's behavior also appear to be predictable and part of the problem?

Tell participants that they have 20 minutes to share their situations together and pick one or two to share with the whole team.

Step 3: The Creative Response

After 20 minutes, get everybody back together in their small groups. Ask the first group to present one of their chosen predictable behaviors that demands a solution. Now give the other three working groups seven minutes to generate a creative, hopefully paradoxical solution for the consideration of the presenting group.

Have each working group in turn offer their creative solutions to the presenting group (Figure 7-13). Suddenly, they will have three or four interesting, creative, and, in some cases, paradoxical solutions to consider. Remember that the problem is often in our solution and is the trigger to more conflict. Our goal is to alter the predictable behavior of the other person with our creative solution and to change our own often-predictable response.

Figure 7-13. Creative Solutions

Suddenly they will have 3 interesting, creative, paradoxical solutions to consider

As the facilitator, comment about the creativity being generated because of the different way of looking at a problem. Make sure the solutions are not critiqued—the best ideas are usually obvious. If you can add perspective to a solution, do so.

Here is a summary of the steps with the timing for each.

Step 1: The Setup	20 Minutes
Step 2: The Directions	30 Minutes
Step 3: The Creative Response	20 Minutes
Total Design:	**70 Minutes**

Questions, Only Questions

Questions, Only Questions (Figure 7-14) is a wonderful design for unblocking a stuck team. We've all been there—experiencing that sinking feeling when the group we are leading is stalled or not functioning on all cylinders, but we can't quite put our finger on the issue. What we do know is that there is tension in the group, that folks aren't relating as they should—there is some kind of unfinished business within the group that appears to be impeding its productivity. Yet there hasn't been any major blowup or crisis, no identifiable issue that shouts to be solved.

Figure 7-14. Questions, Only Questions

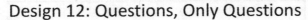

Design 12: Questions, Only Questions

This design will give you a tool to "unstick" your team by helping the team members put their issues on the table, talk honestly without defensiveness, and speak the truth without recrimination—basically, to clear the air.

Step 1: The Setup
One of the best things about this design is that it can be used with little or no notice. No preparation is necessary—all you need is the realization that something is wrong and you should do something about it.

Once you have decided to use this design, the next thing to do is suggest to the group that you have an interesting process that will help move them forward. You can tell them you have done it before, and that it will be engaging and, yes, fun. Then give them these simple instructions:

1. Somebody will begin by asking another person on the team a question that, if answered, would help us explore what's going on in this group.
2. The person receiving the question can only answer with another question—either back at the person asking the original question or at someone else, but it must be a question.
3. The question can be related to the first one asked or can raise a very

different issue. It can be a direct, hard question such as, "Mary, what's keeping us stuck?" or a softball, such as, "Is this making you nervous?" While the meeting participants might look confused, it's actually very simple—and you can give the team a few examples to get them started, as you can see in Figures 7-15 and 7-16:

- Bill asks Mary, "Do you think we have unfinished business that is holding our team back?"
- Mary, instead of responding to Bill, asks Scott, "Do you think everyone is pulling their weight in the group?"
- Scott then asks Mary, "Have you noticed how fast some folks leave at 5 p.m.?"
- Mary then asks Ellen, "Are people free to give each other feedback in this group?"
- Ellen asks Scott, "Why would people not feel free to give feedback to someone in the group?" And so, the process continues.

By giving the sample questions, you are effectively setting a tone and direction for the group. Also ask them to be creative and honest in what they are asking. And remember, this is questions, only questions. We find people can get creative in their questions, such as, "Bill, don't you think we are stuck because we never finished discussing the conflict Mary raised in the group last week?" Then Bill might ask Mary, "Is that true, Mary—how you feel about it?" Thus, a clever question can also be a powerful statement.

Step 2: Identifying the Issues

When you have gone around the team a few times (a lot of questions can be asked in 10 or 15 minutes) and have a pile of issues on the table, stop the process and create an opportunity to focus on some of the issues that have come up. You can put people into random groups of three and tell each cluster to agree on two or three issues that they need to discuss further and attempt to resolve. Or, you can just ask each person to decide on one or two issues that need to be addressed based on the questions and see where there is overlap in their thinking.

Step 3: The "So What"

Capture the issues that arise on flipchart paper, and then have an open discussion in relation to the top one or two only (Figure 7-17). Try to clarify the nature of

Figures 7-15 and 7-16. Sample Feedback Questions

these issues as best you can and collect ideas for possible solutions. Depending on the issues raised, the leap to solutions here can sometimes be a rather large step. If this is the case, you might want to consider using our 6-Step Problem Solving design at this point. If the issues are not too complex or contentious, you can simply hold an open (but time-limited) discussion with the group, after which next steps are outlined.

Figure 7-17. Discuss Top Issues

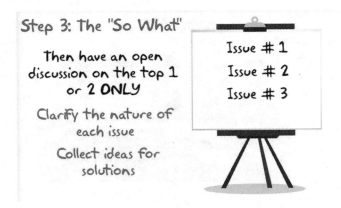

The questions provide a creative way to engage the team members and there's usually a high level of participation. After all, if you are asked a question, you are obliged to ask one in return. Not only that, but behind most questions is an implied statement that needs a response. People tend to become direct very quickly, and patterns of questions tend to arise as the participants feel increasingly open.

Here is a of summary the steps with the timing for each.

Step 1: The Setup	10-30 Minutes
Step 2: Identifying the Issues	5-10 Minutes
Step 3: The "So What"	10-20 Minutes
Total Design:	**25-60 Minutes**

Speak Out

Speak Out (Figure 7-18), the final of our 13 designs, is helpful when dealing with differences between two groups—especially when those differences relate to how people feel treated in terms of ethnicity, race, religion, or gender. How people deal with such challenging issues means digging into the group's culture and usually should not be addressed unless the group is ready to be honest with one another.

Figure 7-18. Speak Out

Ethnicity, Race, Religion, or Gender

Imagine that someone on your team is feeling devalued, which is especially likely when they are in a subordinate position. In our example, it is the women on our team who are feeling devalued by a history of insensitive behavior toward them. Some of the strongly held team norms include don't complain, never cry, stick with the task, and never waste time in the process of how things get done.

In this situation, discounting around gender had been bubbling under the surface for years, but one incident brought the issue to a head: A senior male officer made a highly prejudicial statement in a public meeting; a female counterpart then vigorously confronted him. The remaining women in the room exploded into clapping and laughter, while the men appeared to be in a state of confused silence.

> **TOP TIP** Before getting into the design, remember to keep it simple. Don't try and solve all the unfinished business in a single activity. Making any progress in such a touchy situation can usually be deemed a success, so let's get creative.

Step 1: The Setup

Invite the women of the team (in our example), or the person or group that needs to "speak out," to a meeting and ask each person to develop a 10-minute story about their life—in this case, as a woman in today's world. This means what they love about it, and what frustrates them, angers them, and leaves them feeling diminished. Encourage them to also talk about their experiences as children in their family with respect to the role that (in this case) gender played, and make sure they prepare one piece of advice for the men (or the other group) on the team that they believe will help diminish the issue in the future.

Step 2: The Sharing

Have each member of the "speak out" group share their stories at a deep level with the other women present (Figure 7-19).

Figure 7-19. Sharing Stories

The reason for doing this is to ensure that each "speak out" group member is committed to being honest and to supporting one another as they share their ideas without holding back. For people who usually keep these feelings to themselves, it can be a huge catharsis as each one reveals their strongest feelings, and they are all vulnerable together. It's important that there is no debate, no questioning of each individual's comment other than for clarification.

Step 3: The Big Meeting Invite

After people have shared personal histories and feelings around the issue, arrange a meeting with the whole team (in this case, the men and the women) and set it up as an opportunity to share at a deep level the feelings and history triggered during the incident. The men will probably think that it will be a confrontational meeting with them being the bad guys—but that could not be further from the truth, so try to let them know this. For them, it will primarily be about listening deeply to their female associates and helping the women feel heard.

Step 4: The Positioning

Set the room up with the women sitting together in a semicircle facing the men. Then give the following instructions to the men: These women, their colleagues, have each been asked to share their stories of what it is to be a woman in today's world (Figure 7-20). Each will have up to 10 minutes, and they promise to be honest and specific in the stories and examples they are going to share. As colleagues, they need to understand this history because it has an impact of which they have little understanding. It is not about blame, but about gaining a new understanding of this powerful and unspoken reality. The men's job is to listen deeply and to be open to learning, because later they will be asked to share what they have heard and any feelings they have about it. This is not a debate and it is not about right or wrong.

Figure 7-20. Listen and Learn

Step 5: The "So What"

At the end of the sharing, and after a brief break, have the male members of the team share what they just heard from their female counterparts. Then lead the group in a discussion relating to what this means for them as a team.

The key to this design is to place the men in a noncombative situation, knowing that their responsibility is to listen deeply. For the women, there has to be a commitment to be honest at both an intellectual and emotional level and awareness that they will, as a group, have to be vulnerable. Knowing beforehand that they are aligned with the other women gives the female participants the courage to share their stories in very personal and dramatic ways.

As the design unfolds, the men will begin to hear a reality that they have likely never heard before and understand how this influences their work and their relationships on the team. Again, there is no win-lose aspect to this design, because the focus on both sides is on understanding.

As a follow-up to this design, you might want to arrange another meeting for more in-depth problem solving. A design such as 6-Step Problem Solving would be a good one to generate more detailed strategies for change. Again, you are not expected to solve such an intractable problem. But deep listening is a good beginning. Most likely there are real solutions in the group that a discussion like this can ignite (Figure 7-21).

Figure 7-21. Discussion

It might also be very powerful, at another time, to have the men undertake their own speak-out, because a large part of the problem of gender differences rests in how the men live with huge expectations about what it is to be a man in our society and how that influences their behavior. Once this is done, problem solving in relation to how to establish different "rules of engagement" between men and women on the team or in the organization can be explored with both candor and care.

Here is a summary of the steps with the timing for each.

Step 1: The Setup	10 Minutes
Step 2: The Sharing	50 Minutes

Step 3: The Big Meeting Invite 30 Minutes*
Step 4: The Positioning 60 Minutes
Step 5: The "So What" 30 Minutes
Total Design: **2.5 Hours**
(*between the two face-to-face sessions to set up a meeting invite and proposal with the attendees)

In this chapter, we have shown you four designs dealing with individual or team conflict, with common threads to them. For example, these designs will also help with developing problem-solving skills. The very act of experiencing them will improve the team's communication skills and willingness to speak up. As a result of using these designs, you will also be team building by both dealing with the team's issues (conflict) and engaging the brainpower of the whole team to do this.

Doing nothing is the solution of choice for many teams, so problems tend to fester and keep them from becoming a truly high-performing team. We believe this book, with the focus on intentional facilitation and the use of creative designs, will provide you with a new way of thinking and acting as you attempt to improve your team.

8

OVERCOMING THE CHALLENGES OF VIRTUAL FACILITATION

No matter what industry you work in, you will likely have to work virtually at least some of the time. The push for reducing costs and minimizing expenses is not going away; therefore, the pressure to do more and more without meeting face-to-face will continue to challenge facilitators. In addition, the expanding global nature of many large companies through mergers and acquisitions, increased usage of shared service centers, or companies moving their corporate offices to more tax-favorable locations calls for virtual meetings. On the plus side, facilitators do have an ever-growing number of tools and strategies that can help them work in their growing virtual world.

Common Challenges and What to Do About Them

The most obvious difference about working virtually is that people are not physically in the same place. This creates a variety of challenges for the facilitator.

First, people cannot see one another. There are plenty of funny videos on the Internet that depict the classic conference call: People continually asking, "Who just joined?" and talking over one another, or pregnant pauses waiting for somebody to talk. Virtual participants do not have the visual cues they rely on in face-to-face meetings. This also prevents people from being able to read one another's feelings, so they cannot adjust their approach or accommodate others in the way they might normally. The lack of visual cues makes it particularly difficult to sense the mood in the room.

Second, bad habits that occur in face-to-face meetings get exponentially worse in virtual ones. An example of this is being late—most virtual meetings have participants who join late, either because they are running behind from a previous meeting or they simply lose track of time. Another reason for starting late is because the person hosting is not present on time. Perhaps the fact that people can't see one another in most virtual meetings makes it more acceptable to be late. Or perhaps it's our unconscious minds telling us that it doesn't matter, because the meeting is going to be even more of a waste of time than a regular face-to-face meeting.

Third, people feel so overloaded that they already multitask in face-to-face meetings. When meetings are done via teleconference, it's safe to assume that most of those present do not pay attention and engage in side work on their computers or cell phones. This final example is among the most annoying.

These challenges are just some that confront the virtual facilitator, in addition to those of facilitating a face-to-face meeting. It is therefore even more important to be intentional and creative with your design—not, as many people think, less prepared and structured. You also must be even more selective with the tools that you use for virtual facilitation. There are so many different technologies that it's easy to just use the latest fad file-sharing platform (avoiding pretty much all need for human contact) or feel overwhelmed and not use anything other than email and perhaps a teleconference. The trick is to use your diagnostic mentality to choose the best technology for your situation.

As a rule of thumb, use videoconferencing for all important virtual meetings—ones that require an important decision to be made or require the buy-in of multiple stakeholders. This includes using platforms with screen-sharing capability, like Skype for Business or Zoom. The screen sharing allows everyone attending to collaborate on the same documents in real time and stops all the back-and-forth you get with multiple people editing drafts. Email still works well for sharing documents unless you need to be more collaborative, in which case something like Google Docs is a good option for small groups of people.

There are many books on virtual meetings that go into much more detail than this. However, as long as you are interested in facilitating a great virtual meeting, what follows is really all you need to know in terms of technology, apart from one more important thought: As the complexity of your technology increases, the likelihood of it actually working decreases. Keep it as simple as you can and test it out with plenty of time to spare.

An Example of a Virtual Meeting Design

Here's an example of a meeting we held a few years ago in Paris. We had 13 participants in the meeting room and six virtual participants in four different time zones. We set up the meeting time to try to accommodate the different time zones as best we could, knowing that somebody was going to be up very late or very early. We had videoconferencing capability in the meeting room, one of the virtual participants was in a videoconference room in Mexico, two were in a videoconference room in New York, two were in an office in Japan, and the final one was in his home in California. We made sure that the virtual meeting participants not in videoconferencing rooms could join using their laptop-computer cameras.

We set up the face-to-face meeting room so all the participants could be seen by the videoconferencing camera and split the large screen into four, each showing a live feed from one of the four remote locations. The audio feed was much clearer using the phone line, and we also used screen sharing and instant messaging among all participants.

The purpose of the meeting was twofold: Train the team in administering, scoring, and analyzing a team-building instrument of ours (the Group Management Questionnaire; see *Measuring What Matters* by Rod and co-author Rich McDaniel); and model for the team and its leader the skills necessary for facilitating virtual teams in a focused and experiential manner.

The two-day design began with participants identifying a vision for their team by first sharing what turned out to be deeply personal stories about a great team to which they had once belonged. The key here was to have them identify not only what they did, but what felt truly special about being on that team. We divided them into small groups—two groups of four people and one group of five for the face-to-face participants, and we put the virtual participants together on the screen to make a group of six. The virtual participants all had their own cameras trained on them, and all four locations showing on their screens. This allowed them to talk together without any external facilitation or moderation required.

In their groups, participants began sharing stories of teams from childhood, adolescence, war, and work. They created lists on flipchart paper of what they believed were the characteristics of a great team. In the virtual team, one person was nominated as scribe and trained their camera on a piece of flipchart paper, so the other team members could see what they were writing. (Some videoconferencing software might even allow you to create virtual flipcharts.) We then brought two pairs of groups together and gave them time to develop their collective lists of aspirations (using our Collapsing Consensus design from chapter 5). The virtual team came together on the screen with one of the face-to-face groups. Doing this gave team members a compelling view of what their team could be, and a reason to work together toward this shared goal.

The group then moved to the second part of the design—scoring, analyzing, and interpreting the Group Management Questionnaire (GMQ), a tool for making any shared vision of a high-performing team a reality. This instrument consists of 72 best practices observed in high-functioning teams; the participants either agree they are happening or not. It is quick and easy to use, and was time well spent in getting the individuals over their defensiveness at being imperfect. The results of the team's GMQ, combined with the newly established team vision, allowed the members to recognize a need for strategies for pursuing areas of opportunity that were not currently available to them. Through the art of design and practice of structured conversation, the team began to see what was possible for them as they took their initial steps to closing the gap between their team vision and their current reality (as identified through the GMQ).

By working collaboratively, engaging in dialogue, soliciting needs and issues, and sharing personal stories, participants made sure their input was reflected in the content and expected deliverables for the meeting. Through our design, both the quantity and quality of ideas were at least equal to (or better than) face-to-face meetings, despite the challenges of working virtually.

Virtual Facilitation Can Work

Achieving true collaboration is a challenge in any work environment. In teams working virtually, it can be all the more difficult to attain. This is especially true when team members are practically strangers to one another and are from different cultural backgrounds (as was the case with this team). The key is to build a mutual sense of purpose and focus on the process (the "how" of the work to be accomplished) and the evolving relationships. In any design involving teamwork, there is a need to initially build rapport, to care for how people are treated, and to be sure that participants believe their ideas are valued—even if all of them aren't used.

These ideas, discussed in earlier parts of this book, are foundational for achieving our stated goals in any virtual meeting.

Our example took nearly two days to accomplish, plus a half day of planning. If we estimate that these 19 leaders were valued at $100 an hour, the investment made in our meeting time alone was more than $30,000. Imagine how many similar meetings result in people sitting on the phone for hours, with a few individuals dominating the conversation and others distracted and uninvolved. And that assumes that those facilitating the meeting have some understanding of both the design technologies and the use of modern teleconferencing. But was our meeting worth the money? Without question, yes. And yet, this kind of well-designed initiative remains a rarity in the world of virtual facilitation. The good news is, most of our designs can, with a little creativity, be adapted to virtual meetings.

We talk about having a "design mentality," and that applies to any meeting. Because virtual meetings present meeting organizers with new complexities and challenges, we have found that many people actually do less planning and are less creative. Clearly the first question to doing a virtual meeting right is this: Is the meeting necessary? Is it worth the cost in preparation and execution? Done poorly, and without attention to how to engage those present, the result will predictably be a boring, less than productive use of people's time and energy.

If you understand the fundamentals of any well-designed meeting, having a well-articulated, worthwhile virtual meeting is within your grasp. But, will it require more planning time? Yes. Will it demand some familiarity with how to bring members into the room and into participation? Most certainly. Finally, a commitment to conducting regular, substantive meetings virtually assumes a commitment to investing periodically in face-to-face meetings with these same people. Familiarity with both leaders and participants leads to trust, shared commitments, and the motivation to support one another from a distance so that collaboration, especially between meetings, can be effective.

PART III

NEXT STEPS

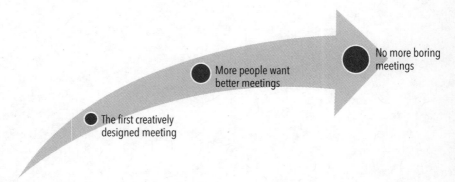

The first creatively
designed meeting

More people want
better meetings

No more boring
meetings

T his final section will prepare you to try out some of the designs and thinking we have discussed throughout the book. So often we hear people
lamenting the fact that most meetings are a waste of time, yet they feel
unable to do something about it. Our mission here is to give you all the tools and
confidence you need to get out there and help us to change meetings—forever.
With your help, we can do this. One meeting at a time.

9

TAKING YOUR
FIRST LEAP

The purpose of this chapter is to prepare yourself to use these materials with your own groups and teams. The 13 designs and accompanying animated videos will guide you in the proper implementation, so please allow ample time to review them and become familiar with all aspects of each design.

Steps to Use These Materials

1. Write down your specific, outcome-based goals for the meeting. These should include task (what needs to get done) and process (how you want people to feel) goals for the group. It's critical to consider what you want the meeting to achieve before setting out with a particular design.
2. Decide which design to choose. We have developed a design selection tool to help you with this (Table 9-1).
3. To help you visualize the design in action, watch the animated video for your chosen design (www.TD.org/NotJustAnotherMeeting). You might even want to watch a couple of videos if there are similar designs you could use. This way you can compare the advantages of each

design side by side. Note that while the animations greatly enhance your likelihood of implementing these designs in your workplace, the detailed design descriptions in chapters 5-7 convey all the necessary steps to successfully facilitate using the designs.

4. As you watch the video, take notes to help you remember important points. You can pause, fast forward, and rewind as necessary.

5. Schedule the meeting.

6. Take any notes with you to act as a script when you facilitate the meeting.

7. Learn with a partner—somebody who is facing the same challenges of facilitating differently, and who can be an advocate for you as you step forward into these new practices.

8. Use your learning partner as a sounding board. Talk through your design ideas, practice with them before the actual event, and plan for things that might go wrong. Having an ally builds confidence and reduces errors.

Even the most skilled facilitators will be in new territory at this point. Most will question their capability and competence—it is a natural part of the process. So, the key is to be easy on yourself. Prepare yourself well and realize that most errors that occur will not influence the overall outcome. There is always something new to learn from any design.

Design Selection Tool

This tool will help to address one of the main challenges people face when starting to use designs in meetings of any kind: their lack of confidence about which design to use. When you are familiar with the designs, this tool will help you make these decisions by comparing the purpose, group size, time required, and minimum trust level for each one.

For the purposes of the tool, we have categorized trust into three groups: not much, some, and a good amount. Trust is a complicated, hard-to-measure commodity. These categories are meant to help assess roughly how much you have in any group, versus how much trust is required for the design to be successful:

- **Not Much:** This is the easiest category, because it covers everything from a brand-new team to one that doesn't talk or even like each other much. Even groups with little or no trust fall into this category, so if you are unsure how much trust there is in your group, use this as your estimate.

- **Some:** This is a team that has been together for some time, works together on a regular basis, and easily engages in social conversation. The members know one another reasonably well and share stories about their families, weekend activities, and so on. With this level of trust, there is likely to be some conflict avoidance and a lack of willingness to raise uncomfortable issues.

- **A Good Deal:** This is a team that has been together for a long time and endured hardship together. It could also be a team that has specifically worked on building trust together with some kind of external facilitation. It is rare to find teams with this level of trust. The members will readily and openly give each other feedback (both good and bad), and they will engage in unrestrained problem solving and debate.

If team or committee members have positive relationships, collaborate effectively with colleagues, directly address conflict as it arises, and give and receive feedback as needed, there is evidence that trust will be steady or on the rise. While there is no valid and consistent measure of such trust, these ideas along with the three levels of trust noted here provide a helpful perspective when considering the use of a particular design.

Let's use an example to illustrate the thinking behind design selection:

Start by writing down your specific, outcome-based goals for the meeting. What do you need to get done (task goals)? Say you want to collect and organize ideas from a group of 12 people. What behaviors, skills, and psychological benefits do you want the team members to come away with (process goals)? You might want every member to feel as if they had their ideas considered as part of the final group decision. You might also want them to learn a new method for putting their ideas on the table.

Next, you need to choose a design. Using the design tool to help with the selection process, first look at which designs will satisfy your task goals. Designs 1, 2, and 3 are all about collecting and organizing ideas. Design 5 also has this as a secondary function. Next, look at group size; with your team of 12 people, all four designs would be suitable.

Next, you look at the level of trust in the group. Say there is some level of trust because you have worked with this group before and know them to be very social together. They still have some reluctance to fully air all their issues together, so they do not qualify for the higher level of trust. With an estimated level of some trust in the group, again all four designs (1, 2, 3, and 5) would be suitable.

Table 9-1. Design Selection Tool

		What Do I Need to Do?	What Else Can the Design Help Me With?	How Many People Do I Have?	How Much Time Do I Have?	What Is the Minimum Trust Level?
1	Future Search	Collect and organize ideas	Problem solving, team building, communication, data analysis, prioritization	10-24	2.5 hours	Not much
2	The Carousel	Collect and organize ideas	Problem solving, team building, communication, data analysis, prioritization	8-30	2 hours	Some
3	Collapsing Consensus	Collect and organize ideas	Problem solving, team building, communication, data analysis, prioritization	4-40	1.25 hours	Some
4	Executives and the Common Person	Strategic planning	Leadership development, feedback, interviewing skills, active listening, data analysis, collaboration	30-3,000	4 weeks	Not much
5	6-Step Problem Solving	Solve a problem	Team building, communication, collaboration, personal growth, collect and organize ideas	1-30	2 hours	Some
6	Kings, Queens, and Fairy Tales	Asses culture	Organization development, conflict, problem solving, collaboration, active listening	5-25	3 hours	Not much
7	Genie in the Bottle	Get feedback	Problem solving, team building, communication, conflict	7-40	3-4 hours	A good amount
8	The 7 in 7	Team building	Active listening, trust building	3-12	30 minutes per person	A good amount
9	The News Conference	Leadership development	Truth telling, vulnerability, active listening, communication, trust building	6-30	2 hours	Not much

	What Do I Need to Do?	What Else Can the Design Help Me With?	How Many People Do I Have?	How Much Time Do I Have?	What Is the Minimum Trust Level?
10 The 8 and 6	Deal with conflict	Problem solving, feedback, team building, communication, personal growth, trust building	2	3 hours	Not much
11 Paradox	Deal with conflict	Problem solving, team building, communication, personal growth, creativity	6-30	1.5 hours	Some
12 Questions, Only Questions	Unstick a stuck group	Organization development, team development, communication, problem solving, trust building, group skills	4-40	25 minutes to an hour	Not much
13 Speak Out	Deal with conflict	Team building, trust building, vulnerability, communication, problem solving, organization development	8-16	2.5 hours	Some

Finally, look at the time required for each design. Because you have been given 1.5 hours in which to achieve your goals, there is now only one design suitable: design 3, Collapsing Consensus. If you think that this design will not deliver on your process goals, one option would be to postpone the meeting until at least two hours are available, so you could use designs 2 or 5 as well. If the group's trust level was at "not much," you would have no choice but to postpone the meeting until 2.5 hours were available, because design 1 is the only one that can be used with a group at this trust level. Please note that it is much easier to adjust time and group size than to increase trust. If you truly needed to increase trust, you would have to use another design first (like design 10 or 12) to specifically work on this aspect.

With your design picked out, you might choose to watch the animated video to get a feel for how it'll look with your team. Although you chose Collapsing Consensus, you might also watch design 2—The Carousel—because of their similarities. After watching the videos and taking notes, if you think that The Carousel is a better fit to achieve your process goals, you might want to renegotiate the current time available up to two hours. In the example here, you decide to stick with the Collapsing Consensus design, because it gives your group members more discussion time for each of their ideas.

Now it's time to schedule the meeting. You send out invitations to all the group members and include a high-level agenda.

Using your notes as a prompt, you feel more comfortable facilitating the meeting. Because you didn't have a learning partner beforehand, you ask a couple of the group members for their feedback once the meeting is over. What did they like about it? What didn't they like about it? How useful was it for them? Did they have any specific feedback on the facilitation? This is always a good idea to start evaluating your performance as a facilitator to ensure your professional development.

Next Steps

One final thought as you transition into trying these designs out: You will inevitably have to deal with one or two difficult people. They might be an obstructionist, or someone who sucks the oxygen out of the room by talking all the time and interrupting others. The design you choose can help to neutralize these difficult people, but how you handle the individual takes the same kind of thinking and preparation as the design for the entire team. For example, using pairs for discussion would be a great way to ensure that the difficult person does not disrupt the entire group. However, you must be prepared to handle the difficult person in the moment to maintain your credibility. As facilitator, the meeting is yours to control and maintain. Setting clear rules of engagement, getting agreement by participants in advance of a problem from members, and then calling out individuals when they are not following the agreed-upon rules of engagement is an essential part of your role. Without an understanding that this is the responsibility of the facilitator, any meeting can be undermined.

10

FACILITATION: ENABLE, ASSIST, EXPEDITE, ACCELERATE

In life and in literature, there has been little effort to differentiate between leadership and facilitation. There are, of course, management functions that require little or no leading, such as organizing and presenting financial statements, or crafting and managing a work schedule for a crew. Design assumes that your impact as facilitator can influence the quality or quantity of the outcome. Thus, enabling people to solve a problem, assisting in the resolution of conflict, expediting the collaborative process, and accelerating movement toward meaningful action are all things facilitators do as they energize both the what and how of work. And these things support the process of getting things done and moving forward. For us, it assumes implementing designs that act as catalysts in the process of doing.

The 10 behavioral abilities in chapter 4 have the facilitator doing something to improve the outcome, the motivation or action of others, using a principle, behavioral skill, or method thought to be essential. While performance management is traditionally a leadership function, it involves the deepest kind of listening and empathy, the clearest feedback, goal setting, and visioning possible. It is the ultimate in facilitation. And conflict will most certainly rear its ugly head along the way. For your purposes, intentionality in each of these behaviors is essential while considering the consequences of your own actions—again, often in real time. All these facilitating actions demand your willingness to scrutinize your own impact in light of your intentions.

The 13 designs in chapters 5-7 provide keys to aid the facilitator in moving the individual or team forward, maximizing their efforts and helping ensure their success. Choosing the right design from the pool is one challenge, as is learning to assess the consequence of your choice. Ultimately, success will be determined by how well you are able to create unique designs that match the assessed needs of any group, meeting, or individual. Like an artist with a palette, you choose creative strategies of engagement that prompt those often silent to speak, bring new ideas to light, and reduce differences so these new ideas can breathe, offering the satisfaction that comes from a truly creative act. Here is portrayed the art of design.

Reading about the 13 designs helps draw you into this essential way of thinking and acting. If you follow these designs with discipline and rigor, we have no doubt they will strengthen you as both a facilitator and a member of the groups and meetings you attend. Practice, with a dash of risk and openness to what is possible, can turn a bland stew into a delightfully tasty meal. We hope you find delectable tastes among these well-crafted designs, with the result being an excited and emboldened facilitator.

ABOUT THE AUTHORS

Rodney Napier

For more than 40 years, Rod has had the privilege and challenge to work with teams and organizations on four continents, in more than 20 countries, and in every conceivable kind of institution, from convents, hospitals, and corporations to the Army Corps of Engineers, the government of Nicaragua, and Outward Bound. He is currently in his 10th year teaching graduate courses at the University of Pennsylvania in conflict management, executive coaching, and planned change. Along the way, he has authored or co-authored a dozen books, including seven editions of *Groups: Theory and Experience,* the seminal text for 20 years in the field of group dynamics; *Measuring What Matters; The Courage to Act;* and the upcoming *The Seduction of the Leader.* His books are theoretically sound, research based, and directed at providing applied, actionable responses to the kinds of problems that regularly face most teams and organizations.

Over the past dozen years, Rod has focused on the skills needed for effective meeting design, along with the strategies that differentiate successful leaders and facilitators from those stuck in the world of predictably boring lectures and PowerPoint presentations. Through the use of videos and animation, Rod and his partner, Eli Sharp, are opening the door for many leaders to a new world of exciting and highly relevant designs and, consequently, meetings of all kinds. In the process they bring years of understanding that almost anyone can now access. All that is required is a willingness to learn, and the courage to risk using new designs and some behaviors that have often lain dormant for many years.

Eli Sharp

Eli Sharp is a recognized expert in Japanese Lean and Six Sigma methodologies. She travels extensively analyzing and improving business, manufacturing, and transactional processes; helping groups work more effectively together; teaching and facilitating teams; and providing coaching to senior leadership.

Integrating process and systems optimization, group and leadership development, and individual executive coaching, Eli provides a holistic strategy to her clients and various techniques to help individuals, teams, and organizations. Her approach is tailored to meet clients' hard and soft needs.

Everything Eli does is grounded in theory. She draws from engineering, business management, continuous improvement, organizational dynamics, and coaching, and works with the practical application of theory, teaching the tools, analyzing complex issues, and making people's lives easier. Her home is at the Gemba—the Japanese term for "real place" or where the work gets done, with the people who do it. She does not preach solutions that lack a real-world context.

Eli has built and led many incredible teams over the past 25 years. She works hard to provide her clients with tools and skills throughout her engagement, so they continue to grow and succeed independently.

Eli has worked in many manufacturing organizations, including hydraulics, food packaging machinery, and medical devices, and has consulted internationally in organizations as diverse as financial services and healthcare provision. She is adept at tailoring her approach to suit different national, organizational, and industry cultures. Her philosophy is to enter the clients' systems with respect and humility, gather data to fully understand the situation and issues from multiple angles, strategize and plan for specific improvements, then help execute the plan, monitor results, and support sustainability.

Eli holds a master's degree in mechanical engineering from the University of Exeter, and is a Chartered Mechanical Engineer. She has an MBA, specializing in operations management, from the University of Plymouth, and a master's degree in organization dynamics (organizational consulting and executive coaching) from the University of Pennsylvania.

INDEX

In this index, *f* denotes figure and *t* denotes table.